WESTMAR COLLEGE LIBRARY

W9-BYS-624

SATHER CLASSICAL LECTURES

VOLUME ELEVEN

1933

ASPECTS OF
ATHENIAN DEMOCRACY

ASPECTS OF
ATHENIAN DEMOCRACY

BY

R O B E R T J . B O N N E R

PROFESSOR OF GREEK IN THE
UNIVERSITY OF CHICAGO

NEW YORK / RUSSELL & RUSSELL

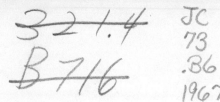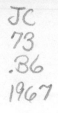

321.4
B716

JC
73
.B6
1967

67570

Copyright, 1933

BY

The Regents of the University of California

REISSUED, 1967, BY RUSSELL & RUSSELL

A DIVISION OF ATHENEUM HOUSE INC.

L. C. CATALOG CARD NO: 66–24671

PRINTED IN THE UNITED STATES OF AMERICA

TO

MAURICE HUTTON

PRINCIPAL EMERITUS OF UNIVERSITY COLLEGE

FOR FIFTY YEARS
CLOSELY IDENTIFIED WITH THE DEVELOPMENT
OF THE HONOURS COURSE IN CLASSICS IN
THE UNIVERSITY OF TORONTO

CONTENTS

CHAPTER I

THE SOVEREIGN PEOPLE

THE ATHENIANS of the fifth and fourth centuries B.C. achieved the most logical form of democracy of any people, ancient or modern. They developed a system which provided for the government of the people, for the people, and by the people. This achievement of democracy was frankly admitted by its opponents. Among the works attributed to Xenophon is a short essay on Athenian democracy. The attribution of the essay to Xenophon is admittedly wrong.

The writer, usually styled Pseudo-Xenophon,[1] begins his description of the means whereby the Athenian masses ruled the city and empire in their own interest as follows:

With regard to the constitution of the people of Athens and their having chosen that particular form of constitution, I withhold praise from them for this reason, that in having chosen that system they chose that the baser sort should be in a better position than the good. For that reason I do not praise them; but once granting that that system has approved itself to them, I shall show that they are effective in preserving their constitution and in carrying out those other arrangements in which they seem to the rest of the Greeks to be at fault.

And in concluding his exposition he says,

Now as to the constitution of the people of Athens, I do not praise the system, but once it has seemed good to them to have democratic rule, they seem to me to preserve it admirably by following the system I have described.

A brief sketch of Athenian constitutional history will be helpful in understanding the development and working of this remarkable system of popular government. In the Heroic Age of Greece, Attica consisted of twelve petty principalities, owing allegiance to the king in Athens. So independent were the subordinate kings that they sometimes made war on one another. Eventually Theseus, a vigorous and shrewd king of Athens, unified Attica politically by depriving the local communities of their independence.[2] Athens became the capital and the seat of government. The people continued, for the most part, to dwell in the country, but there was a considerable centralization of population in the city. The government consisted of the king, his council of elders, and an assembly of the people, the Homeric *agora*. The assembly probably began as a meeting of the warriors of the community. Normally it was summoned by a royal herald to hear proclamations. But it was always a potential instrument for political action by the masses. It was the prototype of the popular assembly or *ecclesia* of democratic Athens.

The aristocracy gradually dissolved the royal authority and prerogatives, and distributed them among annual magistrates. The military power was exercised by a war-lord or *polemarch*. The greater number of the remaining royal functions were performed by the archon, the chief magistrate of the state, while a third magistrate, the king archon, inherited the title and the religious functions of the king. The council of elders was expanded to include the heads of the ruling aristocracy and became the sovereign body in the state. It elected the magistrates from its own ranks. Eventually it came to be called the Areopagus, or the Council on the Hill of Ares.[3]

Soon dissensions arose between the landed aristocracy and the peasantry, who had fallen hopelessly into debt. Civil war was imminent, when wise counsels prevailed and Solon was elected archon. He was named mediator and legislator with a commission to cure the economic ills and reform the constitution. His commission was doubtless confirmed by the assembly. "The rich," says Plutarch,[4] "accepted him readily because he was well-to-do, and the poor because he was honest."

Among the most significant reforms of Solon was the rehabilitation of the popular assembly. It was in all probability called the *heliaea*. All the four classes into which he divided the citizens on the basis of property were entitled to membership. This popular assembly elected the magistrates. Justice continued to be administered by the magistrates, as under the aristocracy, but Solon allowed an appeal from their judgments to the assembly acting as a court.[5] This opportunity for reviewing the verdicts of the magistrates secured a measure of magisterial responsibility to the people. Almost equally important for the future of democracy was the fact that the masses, meeting in the assembly, gained class consciousness and a constitutional channel for expressing their will.

For a generation after Solon there were party struggles, and occasional periods of anarchy, which ended in the tyranny of Pisistratus. Here we get a glimpse of the popular assembly in action. Pisistratus posed as a friend of the people and asked the assembly for a bodyguard to protect him from his alleged enemies. On the motion of one Aristion the request was granted. There was a debate. Solon, according to Aristotle,[6] "opposed the request and declared that in so doing he proved himself wiser than half the people and braver than the rest, wiser than those who did not see that Pisistratus designed to make himself tyrant, and braver than those who saw it and kept silent." As soon as Pisistratus got his bodyguard, he disarmed the populace and established what Aristotle[7] calls a constitutional tyranny.

In dealing with Pisistratus the popular assembly had exhibited no political sagacity or foresight. They were easily deluded and overawed. But the request of Pisistratus shows that the assembly was regarded as a vital element in the constitution, and that the lower classes, by virtue of their numbers, controlled it. This is significant for the future.

During the fifty years of tyranny, the Solonian laws and constitution were nominally in force, but the offices and the government were in the hands of the Pisistratidae and their adherents.[8] Democracy was dormant. With the expulsion of the tyrants it was to be expected that the Solonian system would again become effective. But the nobles hoped for a restoration of the pre-Solonian aristocracy. This was a natural expectation on their part. The tyrants had not been expelled by a popular uprising, but by Spartan intervention, induced by the Alcmaeonidae, a distinguished family that had long been at variance with the Pisistratidae. Consequently Cleisthenes, the leading Alcmaeonid, had hoped for the leadership in shaping the new régime. But Isagoras, with the support of the aristocratic political clubs, undertook the work of reconstruction. Cleisthenes, thus balked in his purpose, embraced the cause of the masses and became the second real founder of Athenian democracy.[9] His success is at once proof of his political sagacity, or rather opportunism, and evidence of the viability of the seed sown by Solon.

The form given to the Athenian constitution by Cleisthenes, his associates, and immediate successors, is in principle substantially the same as the Periclean democracy of the fifth century. From the first it is evident that Cleisthenes had abandoned the Solonian system of balance between the aristocratic and democratic elements in the body politic, and started a movement which eventually resulted in making the popular assembly the sovereign body in the state. And so the constitutional history of Athens during the half-century following the expulsion of the Pisistratidae is concerned mainly with the rise of the assembly to power at the expense of the *boulé*, or council, as it is generally called, the nine chief magistrates, and the Areopagus.[10]

The council was the creation of Solon. It consisted of four hundred members representing the original Ionic tribes of Attica. It controlled the agenda of the assembly. Nothing could come up for discussion or action without a resolution of the council. According to Plutarch,[11] Solon organized the council as a counter weight to the Areopagus; he spoke of them as two anchors for the ship of state.

Cleisthenes effected a thoroughgoing revision of the tribes before he organized the new Council of Five Hundred. In local government, Cleisthenes made fundamental changes. He abolished the *naucraries*, which were mainly administrative divisions of Attica, and organized the *demes*, or village communities, as units of local government. Each deme had an assembly and a *demarch*, or mayor. In a small way they afforded the peasantry an opportunity for gaining some political experience.

In the political struggles preceding and during the establishment of the tyranny the people had been divided into three factions, known as the party of the shore, the party of the plain, and the men of the highlands. Cleisthenes organized the tribes with the purpose of breaking up these old parties. The demes were divided into three groups roughly corresponding to the old political cleavages: first, those of the city and its environs; second, those of the coast; and third, those of the interior. The demes in each of these areas were distributed into ten groups called the *trittyes*; and three *trittyes*, one from each area, constituted one of the new tribes, which now numbered ten. By this system, which has some resemblance to the well-known American device called "gerrymandering," Cleisthenes weakened the power of the nobles and facilitated the democratization of the state. The new tribe ceased to be a geographical unit; it contained men from the city, from the coast, and from the interior. The new council was made up of fifty from each tribe, selected by lot from a large number which were chosen by the demes. The tribal representatives in the council were distributed among the demes proportionately, according to their size. In this fashion the new council was a fairly representative body.

At first Cleisthenes gave the new council much greater powers than those of the Solonian council. Among them was the right to try public offenders and to impose the death penalty. It would appear that the purpose of Cleisthenes, in this measure, was to detract from the prestige and importance of the Areopagus by giving the council a parallel jurisdiction. Under the Solonian system the Areopagus had exercised a wide criminal jurisdiction, including cases of high treason. But the right of the council to inflict capital punishment was very soon withdrawn by Cleisthenes. It is impossible to fix with any certainty the exact date of this change. A very probable date is 502 B.C., when a change was introduced into the oath of the council.[12]

The reason for the restriction of the punitive powers of the council is interesting and important. In the first decade of the fifth century there are references to trials of public offenders before the assembly, which were not appeals from the decisions of magistrates, as provided for by Solon. It is evident that Cleisthenes had soon come to realize that, if the assembly was to be the sovereign body of the state, it must have adequate independent judicial powers. Hence, the criminal jurisdiction of the council was transferred to the assembly.[13] The Areopagus still continued to exercise its ancient judicial powers parallel with those granted to the assembly. Democracy was not yet strong enough to restrict them.

In 487-6 an important constitutional change was made. The lot was introduced into the election of the nine archons.[14] Out of a group of five hundred, nominated by the demes, the archons were selected by lot. The lot was regarded as a democratic device to secure rotation in office. Its introduction even in a modified form at this time was an important step in the development of democracy. Heretofore, with direct election of candidates, the leading men in the state were generally elected to fill the higher offices. In the troublous years between Solon's reforms and the tyranny, the archonship was the chief bone of contention. After the expulsion of the tyrants the office continued to be of great importance, and was regularly filled by leading men. Among them were Themistocles, hero of Salamis, and Aristides, popularly called "the Just." At the same time, the importance of the polemarch as commander of the army was lessened by the election of ten generals by the tribes.[15]

The effect of these changes was to minimize the importance of the magistrates and to increase the importance of the assembly. Leadership in the state must now be sought in the assembly, or in a military career.

As a means of protecting the populace from the restoration of tyranny, Cleisthenes devised "ostracism." Once a year the assembly voted on the question of holding a vote of ostracism. If the decision was in favor of ostracism, at a subsequent meeting in the *agora* each citizen scratched on a potsherd the name of the man who, in his opinion, was a danger to the state. If six thousand[16] or more voted, the man who received a plurality of votes went into exile for ten years without confiscation of property. On the whole it was a simple and sensible protective measure. The only alternative to some such preventive measure was to wait for an attempt at tyranny to be made.[17] This was dangerous, whether the attempt was made by guile or by force. It was better to forestall such moves than to await them. Moreover, it was an important feature of ostracism that, once it was decided upon, the voting was silent and secret. There was no public accusation of any particular man; neither was there any opportunity for ambitious suspects to defend themselves and cajole the people.

The reforms of Cleisthenes elevated the assembly at the expense of the magistrates and the council. The Areopagus alone could compare with it in power and authority. But the Areopagites, recruited from former archons, held office for life, and it was contrary to democratic ideals and principles that a body, whose members held office for life and could not be called to account, should continue to exercise important functions in the state. Moreover, when its membership came to be recruited from the archons, selected without regard to their ability or fitness for office, it was inevitable that it should eventually lose its ancient prestige. But in the meantime, so long as its constitutional powers remained intact, there was always the possibility that the Areopagus would become the center of reaction against democracy. And this is precisely what happened.

The democratic movement, initiated by Cleisthenes, ceased to progress when once its immediate objectives were gained. Meanwhile the Persian war and the founding of the Athenian empire absorbed the popular interest. The Areopagus won such popularity by its services on the eve of the battle of Salamis that Aristotle[18] describes the period between 479 and 462 B.C. as the "Supremacy of the Areopagus." He specifically says that there was no constitutional amendment. The Areopagus simply made use of the powers and privileges that belonged to it, as far back as the time of Solon.

Solon[19] assigned to the Areopagus the duty of superintending the laws, so that it continued as before to be the guardian of the constitution in general. It kept watch over the citizens in all the most important matters, and corrected offenders, having full powers to inflict either fines or personal punishment. . . . It also tried those who conspired for the overthrow of the state.

There is no record of the activities of the Areopagus during the period of its supremacy. But it was not long until democracy began to reassert itself. Ephialtes, the chief democratic leader, began a campaign against the Areopagus by prosecuting many of its members for irregularities in their official and political activities.[20] These prosecutions were doubtless in reprisal for the activities of the Areopagus as *censor morum* and guardian of the state. The next step was to deprive the Areopagus by legal enactments of "the prerogatives from which it had derived its guardianship of the constitution, and to assign some of them to the Council of Five Hundred, and others to the assembly, and the law courts." The date was 462-1. There may be some significance in this date. There is no reliable means of arriving at the average number of Areopagites. But it has been estimated that, in the twenty-five years that elapsed between the introduction of the lot in selecting the archons, in 487, and the attack of Ephialtes, in 462, the entire membership would consist of former archons selected by lot—a much less authoritative group than the elected Areopagites.[21] Ten years later Pericles effected further restrictions. Thenceforth the Areopagus ceased to exercise administrative functions, and its judicial functions were limited almost altogether to the trial of murder cases.

It has been suggested that the poet Aeschylus intended the *Eumenides*[22] as a protest against the attacks on the Areopagus, but inasmuch as he depicts the establishment of the Areopagus by Athena as a murder court, without reference to any political prerogatives, it might just as well be argued that it was intended to support the program of the reformers by showing that the functions they left untouched were its original functions.

The bitterness of the struggle is attested by the assassination of Ephialtes at the hands of the conservatives, and it is a tribute to the liberal ideas and political moderation of the Athenians that the Areopagus continued to enjoy their respect and confidence. On more than one occasion it was entrusted with large temporary powers to execute important political commissions. And when Isocrates[23] wished to advocate a reform of democracy in the fourth century he proposed to restore the ancient supervision of the Areopagus.

Our sources are too meager to enable us to determine just what functions of the Areopagus were turned over to the assembly. It is at least certain that the right to try public offenses exercised both by the Areopagus and by the assembly since 502 B.C. was now exercised exclusively by the assembly. But the greatest gain for democracy was the assurance that there was no longer any political body in the state capable of sharing or restricting the authority of the assembly.

In the struggle with the Areopagus the higher magistracies were further democratized by allowing the archons to be drawn from the *zeugitae*,[24] the third of the four classes into which Solon had divided the citizens on the basis of property. Some time later the *thetes*, the lowest class of citizens, also began to be admitted. The date is not known. In fact, there was no legislation on the subject at all. *Thetes* simply presented themselves for allotment without admitting their status.[25] Evidently this irregularity was winked at by the authorities.

Democracy weathered two dangerous revolutions, in 411 and 403 B.C. The revolutionists on both occasions sought to win the support of moderate democrats by a program of a restricted franchise and the abolition of pay for all but a few officials.[26] But their intention was to establish absolute oligarchy. Upon the failure of the second revolution in 403 B.C. and the expulsion of the Thirty Tyrants, the victorious democrats again showed their patriotism and political sagacity by agreeing to an amnesty for all, except the guilty tyrants.

The oligarchs were crushed; but the moderates again tried by constitutional means to stay the progress of the democracy along radical lines. A bill was introduced into the assembly by a democratic politician to restrict the franchise to landholders;[27] but it failed to pass. Democracy was now firmly established in Athens. Instead of reducing the number of paid officials, they gave a fee of one obol for attendance at the assembly. This amount was soon increased to three obols, the same as the dicast's fee, first introduced by Pericles about the middle of the fifth century. The proposal met with considerable opposition at first. The moderates in the ranks of democracy were still strong. But pay for all public services, especially for members of governing bodies, is indispensable in democracy.[28]

The mixed system of ballot and lot introduced by Cleisthenes was eventually changed to a system by which the lot alone was used for the election of councilors and all magistrates. The date of this change is unknown.

Election by lot was the chief device employed by Athenian democracy for securing the sovereignty of the people. From a modern standpoint, it seems utterly inconceivable that a state should be governed successfully by officials and boards selected by lot. So strong is this feeling that modern writers for a long time refused to believe that the lot was honestly applied.[29] The fact that we have very little information about the actual working of an election by lot, left the way open for much speculation. Moreover, there are occasional charges of irregularities in the use of the lot. But the same charges of corrupt practices are made with regard to the regular elections.[30] Since the recovery of Aristotle's *Constitution of Athens* historians have come to accept the lot as a fundamental feature of Athenian democracy.

The procedure of sortition is not known, and it is of no value to repeat speculations on the point. It is clear that a citizen could offer himself for sortition for any particular office that he fancied.[31] One must suppose that, if volunteers failed, citizens could be drafted for service as officials.

Similarly, there must have been provision for excusing a citizen from service for good and sufficient reasons supported by oath (ὑπωμοσία). The whole purpose of sortition would have failed if citizens could escape service at will. Socrates was councilor in 406. It is difficult to imagine that Socrates of his own accord presented himself for allotment, or that he would have accepted the office if he could legally have refused it. This seems clear from the tone of his reference in the *Apology* of Plato[32] to his membership in the council, and his criticism of sortition as a political device, in the *Memorabilia*.[33]

Sortition was not promiscuous. The following persons were forthwith excluded: those who had been deprived of citizenship; those who had already held the particular office concerned; those who had not yet rendered account for a previous office. Cripples were not permitted to hold any office with which religious functions were associated. All candidates must have reached the age of thirty. These disqualifications and restrictions were matters of record or observation. They could easily be checked up by officials presiding at the election. But there were other disqualifications that could be discovered only by a judicial investigation involving the production of witnesses. Obviously it would be economical of time and effort to defer this inquiry until after the election, and to examine only those upon whom the lot had fallen. This examination was known as the *dokimasia*.[34] The official-elect was required to prove, by witnesses, his citizen descent for three generations, his performance of his duties to his parents and of all military services, the payment of his taxes, the possession of a family tomb, and adherence to the cults of Apollo Patrous and Zeus of the Household. There is no question here regarding a man's fitness for the office. The *dokimasia* was not calculated to secure intelligent and competent officials. It did exclude military slackers, tax-dodgers, undutiful sons, and men of recent citizenship, and those unconnected with the cults especially associated with the family. This was something. On the conclusion of the inquiry anyone was free to show cause in a court of law why the official-elect should not be confirmed in his office. Speeches delivered in three such trials by clients of Lysias are extant. It is evident, from these trials, that the loyalty of the prospective officials to democracy was likely to be called in question. It has been maintained that this was true only in the period after the party struggles connected with the revolutions of 411 and 403. That such is not the fact is suggested by a passage in Aristophanes.[35] In an exchange of accusations and abuse between Cleon and the Sausage-Seller, in the *Knights*, the latter says, "I'll say your father was in the tyrant's bodyguard." In fact, a client of Lysias[36] says that the defendant's whole life was liable to come under review. In practice this is true, whatever may be the theory about sticking to the issue. It is possible that there was a revision of law, after the restoration of democracy, to enable them to exclude *quondam* oligarchs. It was incumbent upon each member of the council, when the *dokimasia* of new members took place before that body, to disclose any evidence he might have that the candidate was unfit for the position.

Not all officials were selected by lot. If an office required technical ability, as in a military office, or diplomatic and oratorical ability, as in an ambassador's office, the candidates were elected. After passing the *dokimasia*, the magistrate-elect took an oath of office and was launched upon his official career.

Some mitigation of inconvenient effects of the lot was achieved by the appointment or selection of assessors or assistants for magistrates and other officials. The archon, the polemarch, and the king archon each chose two assessors. The duties of the assessors are nowhere set forth in the sources. But from the fact that they were required to submit to an audit at the end of the year, it may be inferred that they participated in the administration of the office. It is clear, from an incident related in a forensic oration ascribed to Demosthenes,[37] that one of the reasons for the provision of assessors was to help inexperienced men, selected by lot, to remedy their deficiencies. A certain Theogenes had been selected as king archon. He was of good family, but was poor and "ignorant of business." One Stephanus ingratiated himself with Theogenes by lending him money. Theogenes appointed Stephanus assessor, and married a girl whom Stephanus had represented as his legitimate daughter. Afterwards it appeared that the girl was really the daughter of a courtesan.

The Athenian citizens had opportunities, unequaled in any country or any age, for acquiring political experience. Men who refused to participate in public affairs were generally regarded with contempt, if not with suspicion. Yet, especially after the lowest Solonian class was admitted to the archonship, the vagaries of the lot must have thrust into high office not a few such men as Theogenes, who needed help and guidance even in the routine duties. Because of the care that the Athenians took to render all officials responsible for their official acts, it was desirable that magistrates should make as few mistakes as possible. In matters of official routine the magistrates had also the aid of public slaves who constituted a permanent body of civil servants.

Most elaborate precautions were taken to secure the responsibility of all officials. Ten times annually all officials made a report of their activities, especially where moneys were expended, to the council.[38] A committee examined these reports. If the decision of the council regarding the report of any official was unfavorable, he had the right of appeal to the courts. At the chief meeting of the assembly, in each prytany, the question was put whether the officials were doing their duty. This procedure amounted to recall of magistrates. Any citizen was at liberty to bring charges. If the assembly regarded them as well founded, the official concerned was suspended and put upon trial. Again at the end of the year all officials were subject to a strict judicial scrutiny. Here again financial matters were the chief concern of the examining commissions, but any citizen had the right to file any kind of complaint against an official. If the complainant could make out a *prima facie* case, the official was brought before a court for trial. Considering the wide latitude allowed to prosecutors in Athenian courts, an official might well shrink from the ordeal. Few of the extant forensic speeches deal with litigation arising out of official scrutinies. These deal, for the most part, with exceptional cases, like that dealt with in Lysias' oration against Eratosthenes, one of the Thirty Tyrants, where the special charge was responsibility for the death of Polemarchus, the brother of Lysias, or like that in the speech in behalf of Polystratus,[39] associated with the régime of the Four Hundred.

The numerous references to audits in the orators and in the comedies of Aristophanes clearly indicate that the litigation arising out of them regularly concerned financial dishonesty. But charges of maladministration were quite possible. A favorite trick of the sycophant, as the professional accuser was called, was to attack or threaten to attack an official on his audit. In fact, this trick was his chief stock in trade. Antiphon[40] contemplates the possibility of an attack being made at the audit of a king archon for his refusing to enter a charge of homicide preferred within three months of the end of his tenure of office because he could not conduct the necessary preliminary hearings in the time left.

Originally the nine archons had real powers, political, military, and judicial, but, as we have seen, the introduction of the lot, as a mode of selecting them, marked the end of their political importance. Any reader of the literature of the fifth and fourth centuries B.C., such as oratory, history, and comedy, is struck by the almost complete absence of reference to any of the archons. This is not accident. A perusal of the most detailed description of the functions of these officials found in modern handbooks, giving all the information that can be gleaned from any ancient source, at once reveals the reason. They exercised no real power in the state. The archon was the protector of the family in all its relations and had the chairmanship of courts in all litigation involving the family. He conducted the Dionysia and performed other religious functions. Likewise, the king archon was almost exclusively a religious officer, with legal jurisdiction in homicide cases and a few others. Of the military functions of the polemarch scarcely a vestige remained. He had legal jurisdiction in most of the private suits where one of the parties was not a citizen. All magistrates were specially protected against personal injury during their incumbency of office.

It now becomes clear why the lot, as a device for securing administrative officials, need not be hastily dismissed as a piece of foolishness comparable to the folly of selecting a ship's pilot or a physician by lot.[41] The safeguards insured the selection of men who respected religion, performed their duties to their parents, discharged all their obligations to the state, were not under indictment, and were loyal to democracy. If they were without experience in public business, there were assessors and secretaries to guide them. Some of the officials, such as the Eleven, the Forty, and the Introducers, being members of boards, had the benefit of the experience of their colleagues.

The chief executive body in the state was the council, consisting of fifty from each of the ten tribes, so elected that the demes received proportionate representation.[42] Like all other officials elected by lot, they had to pass a scrutiny (*dokimasia*). This examination was conducted by the retiring council. If one was rejected, he had the right of appeal to a court of law. The council had the right to expel at any time one of its members whom it regarded as unworthy. The final decision, however, lay with a court.

The council was too unwieldy to be effective for the conduct of everyday business. For a tenth of each year, known as a prytany, the work of the council was entrusted to a committee of fifty. They were called *prytaneis*. The fifty members of each of the ten tribes acted as *prytaneis* in order determined by lot. A chairman was chosen for each day by lot. He had the keys to the treasury and the state seal. The *prytaneis* were in constant session during their period of office. They prepared the agenda for meetings of the whole body. The council superintended the warships and dockyards, managed the finances of the state, and received foreign ambassadors. "The council," says Pseudo-Xenophon,[43] "has to deliberate on much relating to war, revenue, legislation, contemporary happenings at home and among the allies; it also has to receive the tribute and look after the dockyards and the temples."

An important function of the council was to prepare the program for all assembly meetings. It was a constitutional rule that no business could come before the assembly without a resolution (*probouleuma*) of the council. In general, the resolution made a specific recommendation regarding the disposal of the matter. Otherwise, it was left to the assembly to act as it saw fit. It might seem that such a rule put too great power in the hands of the council. But the hands of the assembly were by no means tied by the *probouleuma* of the council. The widest possible right of amendment was allowed in the assembly. An entirely new resolution might be substituted. It was enough that the council had put the matter before the assembly. Furthermore, the assembly could pass a motion asking the council to formulate a *probouleuma* on any subject. By this liberal interpretation of the rules, the business of the assembly could be conducted in an orderly manner. And yet it never lost the initiative. Moreover, there was the constitutional provision for the inclusion of certain items of business in the agenda of one or another meeting of each prytany.[44]

In the sovereign meeting of each prytany, in which a quorum[45] was required, there was considered the recall of magistrates, the food supply, the defense of the country, and impeachments. Another assembly was assigned to suppliants. "At this meeting," says Aristotle, "anyone is free, on depositing a suppliant's branch, to speak to the people concerning any matter, public or private." This privilege is analogous to the right of petition in British and American parliamentary practice. Similarly, the other two meetings had their quota of topics that must be brought before the assembly, regardless of the desires of the council. In other words, it was mandatory upon the council to make provision in each prytany for the discussion of specified subjects. This does not mean that they were not free to bring up other matters at these meetings. They could put anything on a program, provided they had also put on that program the subjects specified by law. In this way, the council was prevented from suppressing public consideration of what were regarded as vital matters.

The council continued to be a most useful body in the state, but it remained subordinate to the assembly at all times. The history of the Roman senate shows what power a small compact body can win for itself in a republic. In Athens it was the use of the lot in recruiting the membership of the council that ensured its subordination to the assembly. The lot destroyed continuity. Each year there was an entirely new membership selected from all classes. The proportional representation of the demes drew men together from every part of Attica. This had the good effect

of making it a really representative body. The control of
the council changed ten times each year, as it passed from
tribe to tribe in succession, each prytany.

The council was an efficient governing body. In the
groups of fifty tribal representatives, drawn from the
demes, the chances were good that there would be a percentage of men with some experience in public life. Even
the deme assemblies, limited as were their powers, afforded
some facilities for gaining political experience. In the
council men with qualities of leadership found a place;
they were known as the "orators." In this way the council
helped to develop leaders for the assembly. Ambitious men
might be eager to offer themselves for selection as councilors
for the experience and prestige they would gain,[46] but it was
not at all necessary that a popular leader should ever have
been a councilor.

In the exercise of its judicial functions the council showed
a tendency to overstep the limitations placed upon its
punitive powers. On more than one occasion men were
executed by the council "without due process of law"
(ἄκριτοι). A client of Lysias[47] suggests that the council was
in danger of falling into the habit of disregarding the constitutional limitations on its punitive powers and acting
ultra vires. A few such actions would soon establish a precedent, which succeeding councils might follow. So far as we
know there was no means of preventing the council from
acting ultra vires. Once the victim was executed nothing
could be done. The annual audit would not seem to be a
very effective means of punishing a body of five hundred.

Military officials were not selected by sortition.

In all those offices [says Pseudo-Xenophon],[48] which, when well
filled, bring safety, and when ill filled, bring danger to the whole
state, in those offices the people are not desirous of sharing; they
do not think that they ought to have a share, under the lot, in
the post of general, or in that of cavalry commander, for they

recognize that they are benefited more by not themselves holding these offices, but by allowing those of the highest standing to do so.

This statement would seem to indicate that all military virtue was found in the higher classes. It is, of course, true that the generals were usually men of good family. They were elected, just as the archons were before 487, from the class whose members had advantages in education and experience in public life that were denied to the members of the lower classes. Men of humble origin were not infrequently elected to military offices. But the aristocratic critic, just quoted, chooses to generalize and to assert that where the safety of the state is involved the democracy is ready enough to recognize the superior excellence of the upper class. But Aristotle,[49] speaking of the growth of the democracy after the overthrow of the Areopagus in the middle of the fifth century, says: "As the generals were men of no military experience, who owed their position solely to their family standing, it continually happened that two thousand or three thousand perished in a single expedition." This is, certainly, too high an estimate of casualties,[50] and too low an estimate of the military qualities of the generals, but it does seem to indicate that as much attention was paid to the standing of a candidate in the community as to his military capacity. It was not until the fourth century that the widespread employment of mercenaries developed generals who made a business of war.

The generals had large political powers; they could summon meetings of the assembly and present measures for adoption through the council. They were expected to protect the state against treason and to uphold the democratic constitution.

Athens had no regular diplomatic service. The generals sometimes negotiated treaties and agreements with foreign states. They were charged with the ratification of treaties by oaths and themselves swore regularly as representatives of the people. For special diplomatic missions, envoys were chosen by vote. Here the lot was not used, for skill in speaking, personality, and good social qualities were desirable in a diplomat. These qualities were likely to be found among the upper classes. Dicaeopolis, in the *Acharnians*[51] of Aristophanes, charges that the lucrative posts as members of embassies always go to the scions of the noble families. Turning to the audience, he asks some individuals if they have ever served on embassies. Their names are intended to indicate that they are members of the lower classes. "Come, Marilides, you are old and gray; when have you served as an envoy? *Never.* (He nods.) Yet he's a steady active man. Well, then, Ephorides, Prinides, Dracyllus, have you Ecbatana or Chaonia seen? *Never.* (They nod.)" However, though treaties were negotiated by elected ambassadors and generals, they must always be confirmed by a vote of the assembly. Ambassadors, like other officials, had to pass an audit. The impeachments of Philocrates and Aeschines in 343 B.C. show that the ambassador who betrayed his trust took grave risks. The audit was no empty formality merely having to do with an expense account. It included a thorough examination of the foreign policy involved.

Modern investigators of Athenian political history, particularly during the Peloponnesian war, have pointed out that there was a war party and a peace party. This is a natural situation in a long drawn out war. The significant factor in the situation is the election of the generals. By studying the political affiliations of the men elected each year, it has been possible to determine the relative strength of the two parties year by year. In a sense, the freedom of decision on the part of the assembly was thus restricted. The policy was to some extent determined for a year by the election of generals. If the war party won the election the board of generals would naturally prosecute the war vigorously and, personally or through the party henchmen in the assembly, work for the rejection of peace proposals from the enemy, or nullify peace propaganda in the city. There was always a tendency on the part of an ambitious and aggressive general to ally himself with a strong political leader, so as to secure support for his war measures. But in spite of virtual commitments for a policy of peace or war, the Athenian *ecclesia* was a primary assembly which met frequently and reacted instantly to public opinion. No political platform, however expressed, or board of generals, could bind the assembly or determine its actions.

In the field of foreign policy, it is true, certain traditional attitudes were always present. For example, Athens had to import the major part of the grain she consumed. This supply could only be ensured by a strong fleet. Sea power must always be a vital factor in Athenian naval policy. And the man in the street knew it.

Administration of justice constituted an important part of Greek government. The assembly itself could, by means of impeachment, administer criminal justice and frequently did so in the case of unusual and serious offenses which are described in Greek sources as "new" and "unwritten" because they were not found in any criminal statute. In certain cases impeachment before the assembly was mandatory, according to the so-called impeachment law cited by the orator Hypereides[52]—for example, high treason, betrayal of the military forces, or of a fortress.

Xenophon reports Socrates as pointing out the folly of selecting public officials by lot. "None would choose a pilot, or builder, or flutist by lot, nor any other craftsman for work in which mistakes are far less disastrous than mistakes in statecraft." But this is not a valid criticism, because, as we have seen, the officials elected by lot did not govern Athens. Isocrates'[53] only objection to the lot is that men hostile to the democracy might be elected to office.

True. But such candidates, if known, could easily be rejected at the *dokimasia*. He approves the mixed system of election and sortition which was introduced by Cleisthenes. Pseudo-Xenophon[54] approves the lot as a democratic device, but disapproves democracy as a form of government. And Aristotle[55] says explicitly that "the appointment of magistrates by lot is democratical, and the election of magistrates oligarchical."

Pericles, in the funeral oration reported by Thucydides,[56] expresses his faith in the political capacity of the multitude. "An Athenian citizen does not neglect the state because he takes care of his own household. . . . We alone regard a man who takes no interest in public affairs, not as a harmless, but as a useless person; and if few of us are originators, we all are sound judges of a policy." But Pericles is idealizing Democracy as he saw it when it was at its best.

Aristotle raises the question whether, in a state, the one best man, or all, should decide where the law does not determine.

According to our present practice, assemblies sit in judgment, deliberate, and decide. Now any member of the assembly, taken separately, is inferior to the wise man. But the state is made up of many individuals. And as a feast to which all guests contribute is better than a banquet furnished by a single man, so a multitude is a better judge of many things than any individual.

Others took a different view. The prevalent anti-democratic attitude is well expressed by the apocryphal story of Anacharsis, the Thracian traveler, a contemporary of Solon. After visiting a meeting of the Athenian assembly, he is reported to have said that he was amazed to find among the Greeks that the wise advised but the fools decided.[57]

This discussion of the growth and development of the political power of the Athenian assembly may be fittingly closed with the words with which Aristotle[58] concludes his account of the eleven constitutional changes in Athenian history: "The Democracy has made itself master of everything by its votes in the assembly, and by the law courts, in which it holds supreme power." The origin and development of the law courts, and the manner in which democracy gained control of the administration of justice will be treated in the next chapter.

CHAPTER II

THE JUDICIARY

THE JUDICIARY, as a branch of government, played a much more significant rôle in Greek city-states than it does in modern communities. When the artificer of the famous shield of Achilles, described in the *Iliad*,[1] wished to portray typical scenes of Greek public life, he chose as one of them, not an executive council in session or an assembly legislating, but a group of elders administering justice in the market place. Always in their aspirations and struggles for political liberty the first concern of the Greeks was for justice. They believed that the assurance of justice to its members was the first duty of the state. Thus, when Plato constructed his ideal state in the dialogue which he entitled *The Republic*, the subtitle of the work was *Concerning Justice*. "Equality before the law" (ἰσονομία) was the watchword or slogan of ancient democracy, rather than "Liberty" (ἐλευθερία).

After all, this was but a natural attitude, for people cannot work in harmony if conflicting claims and disputes are not satisfactorily settled and public offenders duly punished. This was particularly true in a Greek community, where citizens were expected to coöperate closely in the everyday service of the state.

The story of the administration of justice in the western world begins with the arbitrator. In the Heroic Age, as pictured by Homer, there was no judiciary. Disputes that did not result from deeds of violence were brought before an arbitrator by agreement. Such cases in modern systems would be normally classified as civil suits. A reluctant disputant was often induced to arbitrate by a challenge to lay a wager. Thus in the famous trial scene described in the *Iliad* each litigant has deposited a talent to be paid to the winner.[2] Naturally, arbitrants sought the services of a man of integrity and impartiality. The prestige of the king marked him as the natural arbitrator. This is the reason why Aristotle says[3] that the Heroic kings were judges.

Whomsoever [says the poet Hesiod][4] the Muses, the daughters of Zeus, see fit to honor, beholding him sprung from the loins of Zeus-born kings, upon his tongue they pour the sweet dew, and forth from his mouth flow honey-sweet words; upon him all the people gaze as he gives binding decisions, clear and just. This man, with his knowledge and sureness of speech, can abate in a moment even the mightiest contention. For to this end were kings granted wisdom, that they might bring redress in the market-place to men of the people who suffer wrong, quietly and easily, persuading them with gentle words. As he walks to and fro in the city they seek his favor as they would a god's, softly and reverently, and his head is held high in the assembly.

This picture is not drawn from the life that Hesiod knew (cf. *Works and Days*). It depicts, rather, the ideal royal arbitrator of the Golden Age.

It was in the interest of the aristocratic government that succeeded monarchy to facilitate recourse to arbitration. This could easily be done by arranging for more or less regular sittings in the market place for the convenience of arbitrants.[5] Out of these, in the course of time, grew compulsory processes of law and regular courts. The first step was to make arbitration obligatory. Arbitrants soon began to give gifts in kind to the arbitrators. The proof is found in the epithet "gift-devouring" (δωροφάγοι) applied by the poet Hesiod[6] to the royal judges in Boeotia. Once the business of settling disputes became profitable to the rulers, voluntary arbitration soon hardened into compulsory arbitration. Under the aristocracy that followed the Heroic kingship, arbitration was one of the regular functions of government. It was not conferred upon the magistrates by law, for as yet there were no codes or constitutions. The compulsion was the product of custom, precedent, public opinion, and the self-interest of the ruling aristocracy. Obligatory arbitration differs from a compulsory process of law because the arbitrator strives first to effect an equitable settlement, whereas the judge pronounces a purely legal judgment.

Criminal law arose from the natural instinct of a community to protect itself against internal foes as well as external enemies. Men who by their acts endangered the security and peace of the community were regarded as public offenders, and were dealt with by the most representative public body in the state.

In the Homeric communities the public meeting of citizens, called the *agora*, passed and executed community judgments. Anyone could summon it.[7] On occasions of great excitement the populace hastened to the market place without a summons. When news of the slaughter of the Suitors was spread abroad, the people of Ithaca assembled of their own accord and put Odysseus on trial.[8] Such actions are really instances of community self-help. Some scholars[9] have hastily dismissed them as "mob violence" and "lynch law." But this is a mistaken view.[10] It is only when functions of properly constituted courts are usurped that we can speak of a "lynch law." In ancient Greece, if either the king or his council wished to punish a public offender, the only course, so far as is known, was to summon the people, put the matter before them, and let them take what measures they saw fit to punish the wrongdoers. Fines, banishment, and death by stoning were the usual forms of punishment in primitive times. This type of criminal justice, administered by the assembly, reappears in Athens after the reforms of Cleisthenes.

Athens had the credit of being the first city in Greece to establish regular legal processes.[11] In Athens under the monarchy it may be confidently assumed that much the same system of settling disputes and punishing wrongdoers prevailed as is pictured in the Homeric epics. But when annual magistrates—archon, polemarch, and king archon —took the place of the hereditary monarchs, there are indications that the new government—aristocracy—made provision for the administration of justice. The annual archon goes back to the early seventh century, 683-2 B.C.[12] His proclamation,[13] upon his taking office, guaranteeing security of property to the citizens, implied some kind of legal process. For if anyone was deprived of property by force or by fraud, and appealed to the archon for restitution, an official inquiry would be necessary to enable the magistrate to establish or dismiss the claim. Such an inquiry, with witnesses and parties summoned before the magistrate, would in effect be a process of law.

Further proof that legal processes were in use in Athens in the seventh century is found in the appointment of six junior magistrates, called *thesmothetae*, in the middle of the century. The *thesmothetae*[14] seem to have been instituted to relieve the other magistrates of increasing judicial work and to record all judicial decisions, including their own; but there is considerable dispute as to their exact functions.

At first there were no written laws. Rulers and magistrates administered an unwritten customary law, which could be interpreted and modified to suit the interests of the ruling class. Soon judges were charged with accepting bribes and giving what the poet Hesiod calls "crooked decisions." It was an easy step from gifts to bribes. The dissatisfaction of the masses took the form of a demand for written laws with prescribed rules of procedure and fixed punishments. Of the despotic ruler and judge, Euripides in the *Supplices*[15] says:

> But one rules, keeping in his private hands
> The law: so is equality no more.
> But when the laws are written, then the weak
> And wealthy have but equal right.

Codification of laws became general throughout Hellas in the course of the seventh century, when writing had become widely diffused. In Athens Draco formulated a code in 621 B.C. It was notorious for its harsh punishments. Demades, a contemporary of Demosthenes, with a knack for phrase-making, said that Draco's laws were written in blood.

Only the homicide laws of Draco have survived. The others were soon repealed. In the Heroic Age the murderer was not regarded as a public offender. If he escaped death at the hands of his victim's relatives, he either paid a blood price or went into exile. Neither the authorities nor the general public were concerned with the matter. But in time the notion that homicide involved pollution forced the government to take action, because the pollution affected all who came in contact with the murderer. The action took the form of a trial to determine the guilt or innocence of the accused who elected to stand his ground. Another motive for state interference was the danger that blood feuds might threaten the security of the state itself, where powerful families were involved. It cannot be determined with any degree of accuracy just when state intervention began. Suffice it to say that the semi-religious ritualistic procedure of homicide trials found in Draco's laws is not his invention. He evidently put in writing traditional practices that were in current use. In early times the distinction between different kinds of homicide were not drawn. The Areopagus, which was reputed to be the most ancient homicide court in Greece, tried all cases.

But in Draco's code[16] appears the classification of homicide as voluntary, involuntary, and justifiable, though the sections dealing with voluntary or premeditated homicide are not extant. In addition to the Areopagus there were four minor homicide courts. The court of the Palladium tried cases of involuntary homicide, while the court of the Delphinium tried cases of justifiable homicide. These courts, in all probability, were instituted to try homicides who took refuge in shrines, claiming justification. It was inconvenient to assemble the entire Areopagus, so a committee, or commission, of fifty-one Areopagites was sent out to try such cases. They were called *ephetae* and were under the chairmanship of the king archon. The number was odd in order to avoid a tie vote. A court at Phreatto, also composed of *ephetae*, held sessions on the shore. It heard the plea of a man accused of another homicide while in exile for homicide. The accused made his plea from a boat moored offshore in order that he might not pollute the soil of Attica. The fifth court, the Prytaneum, was a purely ceremonial court for the disposal of animals and objects that had caused the death of human beings. Like *deodands* in old English law, they were cast beyond the bounds of Attica. This court also pronounced the interdict against unknown homicides, forbidding them to frequent public places. It consisted of the kings of the tribes and the king archon.

But the ills and abuses from which the Athenian masses suffered could not be cured by a legal code. In 594 B.C. Solon was entrusted with the task of finding a solution for the political and economic troubles and restoring harmony in the state. Only the legal reforms of Solon need concern us here.

Under the aristocracy the magistrates had "the power to decide cases finally on their own authority."[17] Under the Solonian constitution the magistrates continued to perform their judicial functions, but their verdicts could be appealed to a popular court known as the *heliaea*. The purpose of this innovation was to enable the lower classes, who by their numbers dominated the *heliaea*, to safeguard their rights and privileges under the new constitution against the attempts of the magistrates to nullify them in individual cases by "crooked decisions." Data regarding the membership and organization of the *heliaea* are meager. All four classes of citizens were eligible for membership. The popular courts or dicasteries of the fifth century were most certainly derived from the Solonian *heliaea*. Aristophanes frequently calls the dicasts, *heliasts*. Owing to the fact that the dicasteries were drawn from a body of six thousand citizens selected annually by lot from citizens of thirty years and over, it has been too hastily assumed that the *heliaea* also was composed of a limited number, possibly six thousand, selected in the same fashion.[18]

The chief characteristics of a judicial body, as distinguished from a legislative body, are an oath and a secret ballot. In later times the six thousand dicasts took an oath of office annually in a body. The fact that the oath was called "heliastic" would seem to indicate that it goes back to the time of Solon, when the *heliasts* functioned as a body. Of an age qualification in the time of Solon there is no trace. It seems likely that the popular assembly and the popular court were one and the same body. When acting as a court, the citizens took an oath and voted secretly. In Doric states in Greece ἁλία or ἁλιαία is the common word for a public assembly. There is undoubtedly some linguistic relation between ἁλιαία and ἡλιαία, but its exact nature is still undecided. The *heliaea* of Athens, then, is doubtless the resuscitated *agora* or popular assembly of the Heroic Age, which did duty both as an assembly, like the later assembly, and as a court of appeal. Owing, perhaps, to the greater importance of the judicial powers, the name *heliaea* came to be restricted to the assembly acting as a court.

Another significant democratic feature of the Solonian system was an innovation in the prosecution of cases in court. Heretofore only the victim of an injustice could prosecute. Now the privilege was extended to all citizens in certain specified cases. Aristotle describes it as "the right of every person who so willed to claim redress on behalf of anyone to whom wrong was being done."[19] These words suggest acts of violence against the person, such as we now regard as crimes. But they are too indefinite to enable us to make a list of the wrongs that could be redressed by a volunteer accuser. In fact, it seems that Solon did not attempt to define the kind of wrong he had in mind, but simply added a general prosecution clause to every statute providing pains and penalties for wrongful acts.[20] This provision laid the foundation of criminal law, because it is based cn the idea that certain types of wrongdoing are prejudicial to the community as well as to the victim. But Solon's immediate object was rather to insure law enforcement in the interest of the lower classes. The wealthy or well-born wrongdoer could not escape prosecution by threatening or bribing his victim, nor hope for a favorable verdict by collusion with a magistrate in sympathy with the upper classes. Any citizen was a potential prosecutor, and every citizen was a member of the court of appeal.

The Areopagus continued to act as *censor morum* and a court for the trial of public offenders. "It kept watch over the citizens in all the most important matters, and corrected offenders, having full powers to inflict either fines or personal punishments."[21] The new constitution was protected by a law providing impeachment before the Areopagus for those who conspired to overthrow the state.[22] The verdicts of the Areopagus were not subject to appeal.

Upon the expulsion of the tyrants in 510 B.C., Cleisthenes, a scion of the famous Alcmaeonid family, put himself at the head of the populace and laid the foundations of Athenian democracy. One of the earliest measures of reform was the granting to the popular assembly of inde-

pendent legal jurisdiction in cases that lay beyond the
jurisdiction of the magistrates.[23] Under the earlier political
systems these cases had been tried by the Areopagus. The
next step of the growing democracy was to make the *heliaea*
a court of first instance for all cases, instead of a court of
appeal.[24] It is obvious that a huge popular court could not
handle all the litigation of a city like Athens and its growing empire. So the difficulty was met by selecting six thousand citizens by lot from those of thirty years and more.
These were divided into sections of five hundred and assigned to the various magistrates and boards, possessing
judicial powers, to try cases under their chairmanship. These
sections were called dicasteries and they bear some resemblance to modern juries. But there are so many differences
that the comparison, though convenient, is apt to be mis-
leading.

This innovation practically abolished the legal jurisdiction of the magistrates. They retained the right to inflict
summarily a small fine upon those who disobeyed their
commands or interfered with the performance of their official duties. This power is analogous to that of the modern
judge to punish recalcitrant persons for contempt of court.
Within their respective jurisdictions the magistrates accepted and prepared cases for trial like a modern court
clerk, and presided at the sessions of the court like a chairman. But neither of these functions involved any real judicial power. If an ill-advised suitor came to the wrong court
to institute legal proceedings, the magistrate would put
him right. In court the magistrate saw that the proceedings
were conducted according to law. Unlike the modern judge,
he had no influence on the verdict. The dicasts determined
both the facts and the law in the case.

The dicasts numbered six thousand because for certain
purposes a quorum of six thousand in the assembly was
required, as in votes of ostracism.[25] Thus the dicasts, as a

body, represented the whole people, and by a curious and convenient legal fiction this representative character was extended to each dicastery. The dicasts' fitness for office was not tested in any way, nor were they, like the magistrates, held accountable for their acts. There was no appeal from their verdicts. The dicasts were not, like the magistrates, the servants of the people; they were the people. This is what a fifth-century writer[26] means when he says that, in Athens, cases were tried by the people.

The grant of independent judicial powers to the assembly and the institution of popular courts laid a firm foundation for democracy, but the Areopagus had still to be reckoned with. As a council it went back to the Homeric council of elders, and constituted the sovereign body of the state under the pre-Solonian aristocracy. As a homicide court it had an ancient and honorable history.[27] The reforms of Cleisthenes had not explicitly restricted the judicial powers of the Areopagus. But the expansion of the jurisdiction of the assembly naturally involved considerable diminution of the activities of the Areopagus. For example, traitors and subverters of the constitution had been tried by the Areopagus under the aristocracy, but when the assembly gained the right to try public offenders, state trials before the Areopagus fell into abeyance. For instance, Miltiades, the hero of Marathon, was charged with injuring the state by an ill-advised expedition against the island of Paros. He was not tried by the Areopagus, but by the assembly.

But this situation did not satisfy the rising democracy. The judicial powers of the Areopagus might at any time be used in the interests of the conservatives to the injury of democracy. According to Aristotle's account,[28] the Areopagus intended to bring to trial Ephialtes, the democratic leader, who was preparing to restrict its political powers. This action on the part of the conservative Areopagus precipitated a political crisis, and Ephialtes and his associates were able to put through their program and reduce the Areopagus to a homicide court.

Ten years after the first attack upon the Areopagus, Pericles ended the campaign in 452-1 B.C. by substituting five hundred dicasts for the fifty-one *ephetae* who sat in the minor homicide courts. As the *ephetae* were commissions drawn from the members of the Areopagus, this legislation was virtually a further restriction of the judicial powers of the Areopagus.[29] Owing probably to religious conservatism, the name *ephetae* continued to be used. By these various measures the whole of the administration of justice, with the exception of trials for premeditated homicide, came definitely and finally under the jurisdiction of the assembly and the heliastic courts.

The guardianship of the laws, which had long been a prerogative of the Areopagus, was vested in the heliastic courts as far as possible. Illegal or unconstitutional legislation could be annulled by an indictment known as the *graphe paranomon*.[30] The right of the Areopagus to see that the magistrates administered the laws was no longer of much importance, since the magistrates ceased to be independent judges. But the votes of confidence in each prytany and the annual scrutiny enabled the assembly to deal with any infraction of laws by a magistrate.

Similarly, the censorship of morals was allowed to lapse. It may have been found necessary to pass laws providing punishment by process of law for acts which the Areopagus had punished by virtue of its censorial power in arbitrary fashion "without assigning the reason for the punishment." A possible example of this kind of legislation dealing with personal misconduct was the law under which Aeschines prosecuted Timarchus for speaking in the assembly after being guilty of squandering his patrimony and prostituting his person. Or the existing forms of action might be extended to take cognizance of such acts. The trial of Aspasia for impiety about 432 B.C. is a case in point. It would seem that offenses against public morality could be combined with a charge of impiety. In the case of Aspasia, the subjoined charge was "contributing to the delinquency of free women." Still other offenses against public morality or religion could be dealt with, as the need arose, by means of impeachment before the assembly. An example was the impeachment of Anaxagoras under the decree of Diopeithes about 430 B.C.,[31] directed against those who disbelieved in the gods or sought a physical explanation of the universe. In these and similar ways the indefinite censorial powers of the Areopagus were virtually exercised by the assembly and the heliastic courts.

There are indications that the assembly, in the latter part of the fifth century, fell into the habit of turning over to the courts impeachments that were first lodged in the assembly. Philocleon, the old dicast portrayed in the *Wasps* of Aristophanes,[32] magnifying the power and prestige of the heliastic courts, says:

> And if ever the Council or People have got a knotty and
> difficult case to decide,
> They pass a decree for the culprits to go to the able and
> popular Courts to be tried.

The records of fifth-century litigation are too meager to enable us to test this view fully. Pericles was tried for peculation, not by the assembly, as one might have expected, but by an extraordinary court of fifteen hundred in 430 B.C. But when public indignation was really aroused, as it was by the failure of the generals to pick up the shipwrecked sailors after the battle of Arginusae in 406 B.C., the assembly itself tried the generals.

But there was a marked change in the fourth century. So many cases, even the most trivial, were tried by the assembly, that the orator Hypereides[33] protested vigorously against the practice. For example, men charged with paying more than the maximum wages to flute-girls were impeached before the assembly. There were some advantages in an impeachment before the assembly. There were few technicalities and delays. And, what was a matter of great importance, the rule requiring the plaintiff to pay a fine of one thousand drachmas if he failed to obtain at least one-fifth of the votes, did not apply in cases before the assembly.[34]

Pay for the dicasts was instituted immediately before the reforms of Ephialtes.[35] One of the principal motives for the measure was to gain popular support for the new democratic movement, started by Ephialtes and Pericles, which culminated in the elimination of the Areopagus as a possible rival of the assembly and the heliastic courts. Pay for jury service was first suggested by Aristides, the founder of the Athenian empire, as a means of distributing the profits of imperialism among the lower classes.[36] They were urged to come to Athens and engage in paid state service. Pericles, it is said, was induced by his political necessities to undertake the reform. Being a poor man, he was unable to cope with Cimon, his wealthy and liberal opponent, and seized upon the suggestion of a political friend that he subsidize the people with public funds. This was euphemistically termed "giving the people their own." This was the last step in the democratization of the law courts. Members of the lower classes were now freely able to volunteer for jury service.[37]

In the fifth century a panel of dicasts was assigned to a particular court, where they continued to sit throughout the year.[38] They numbered five hundred, but the court, like the council, could function with fewer than five hundred.[39] The fixed personnel of the court made it possible to bribe dicasts on a large scale. Attention was drawn to this danger by the sensational exploit of Anytus, who bribed a whole panel.

This system lasted until the restoration of democracy in 403 B.C., after the rule of the Thirty. To meet the difficulty caused by fewer available dicasts, the number in each court was in certain circumstances reduced from five hundred to four hundred and one, or two hundred and one. This device had already been suggested to furnish more courts, and thus to relieve the congestion of litigation in the fifth century, but it did not find favor because of the danger of bribery.[40] Now, however, precautions were taken to make bribery practically impossible. The dicasts were divided into ten sections, and each section was assigned to a court by lot as required. A system of plural registration enabled a man to belong to two sections at once. This system made it possible to secure a full quota for each court, and an odd number was drawn so as to avoid a tie. About the middle of the fourth century, the method of recruiting and drawing dicasts was again changed. The plan described by Aristotle was extraordinarily intricate.[41] The object, apparently, was to make bribery wholly impossible.

Athens had no public prosecutors, such as the crown attorneys and state's attorneys of British and American systems. Solon permitted anyone to prosecute a wrongdoer, because he believed that "the best governed state was that in which those who were not wronged were no less diligent in prosecuting wrongdoers than those who had personally suffered." No change was made by subsequent reformers. Justice continued to be administered on the initiative of volunteers. It was the policy of Athens to rely upon the citizens for all sorts of public services that are performed in modern communities by elected or appointed officials. On occasion, where important public interests were involved, advocates were appointed to take care of them, but the volunteer was not prevented from assisting. Indeed, he was encouraged to do so.

There developed from the system of volunteer accusers introduced by Solon certain abuses which seem to us serious. In certain types of cases, prosecutors were encouraged to take action by the prospect of receiving a percentage of the moneys recovered by the state, or of the fines levied. Personal and political foes were not slow to seize upon opportunities for revenge by lodging criminal charges. The resulting litigation often developed bitterness and litigious feuds. The prosecutor in such cases did not scruple to announce his enmity, confident of public approval. Lycurgus,[42] the most impartial and conscientious accuser in Athenian legal history, believed that it was the duty of a good citizen to regard as personal enemies those who were guilty of wrongdoing to the state. It was, according to Aeschines,[43] a commonplace that "personal or private enmities rectify many public wrongs."

The Athenians of the fifth and fourth centuries devoted so much time to litigation that their litigiousness became proverbial. Aristophanes never wearies of jesting about their preoccupation with litigation. "Grasshoppers chirp upon their boughs a month or two," says one of the characters in the *Birds*,[44] "but our Athenians chirp over their lawsuits their whole life long." Pseudo-Xenophon,[45] the late fifth-century critic of democracy, in this connection points out that, owing to the press of court business and the multitude of festivals, during which all business was suspended, the courts were heavily congested. "How could it be otherwise," he asks, "seeing that they have to decide more private and public lawsuits than all the rest of the world together? Even now, when the courts sit throughout the year, they do not suppress crime because of the size of the population."

Much of the daily litigation in Athens originated in provisions in the Athenian political system which are unknown in modern states. There were also peculiar features in the legal system which tended to encourage the litigious spirit. An examination of these features of the Athenian legal and political system will help to explain, if not to justify, the Athenian preoccupation with litigation.

A favorite form of punishment in ancient communities was to deprive convicted persons, either wholly or partly, of their political and civil rights. The curious variety of these penal disabilities in Athenian practice may be seen in a partial list preserved by the orator Andocides.[46] They include the deprivation of the right to speak in the assembly, to be a councilor, to bring public suits, to enter the market place, to sail the Hellespont or to Ionia. These and other similar penalties often required further litigation for their enforcement. There was no police force to keep track of persons thus convicted and see that they observed the restrictions. The state had to rely on volunteer prosecutors. Anyone discovered exercising these forbidden rights was liable to summary arrest, trial, and further punishment. The number of persons suffering from these disabilities was so considerable that it was thought worth while to grant them amnesty in times of great national danger.

The Athenian courts were regularly called on for services that have no parallel in modern states. This was important for democracy, as it enabled the people to participate more fully and effectively in the public administration and to achieve that control of the state which Aristotle emphasizes more than once.

Athenian magistrates-elect were required to establish at a scrutiny, known as a *dokimasia*, certain required qualifications for office. The nine archons- and councilors-elect appeared before the council. If they were disqualified by the council, they had a right of appeal to a court. Other officials appeared in the first instance before a court. Any citizen was permitted to bring charges against the candidate at this time. The inquiry covered a man's whole career. When the lot fell upon Demosthenes for the council, his enemy Meidias seized the opportunity to bring an accusation against him. The nature of the charge is not at all clear. It may have been manslaughter. Normally, the *dokimasia* passed off as a mere formality, but in the generation that followed the oligarchic revolutions of 411 and 404 it was not unusual to charge candidates with participation in, or sympathy with, the revolution. The expansion of the powers of the courts is seen in the fact that originally the council of five hundred conducted the *dokimasia* of councilors- and archons-elect "with full power to reject candidates for office as unsuitable, but now," says Aristotle, "these have a right of appeal to the law courts."[47] A rejected candidate suffered no penalty beyond rejection.

A magistrate, during his year of office, was subject to recall by action of the assembly. At the principal meeting of the assembly in each prytany during the year, an item in the agenda was a vote to "ratify the continuance of the magistrates in office if they were performing their duties well." If the vote was unfavorable to an official, he was suspended and at once brought to trial for malfeasance in office.

But the chief investigation into the official acts of magistrates and all other officials came at the end of the year. An elaborate procedure was devised for the scrutiny of the conduct and accounts of outgoing officials. A board of thirty, made up of ten *logistae*, ten *euthynoi*, and ten *synegoroi* examined the accounts.[48] If these officials were satisfied, the outgoing magistrate was sent before a popular court with the recommendation that he receive his discharge. But any citizen could at the court session bring charges and show cause why the discharge should not be granted. If, however, the board of inquiry found evidence of wrongdoing, the case was at once referred to a court for trial. Opportunity was given to any citizen for laying charges against the retiring official. The *euthyna*, as this investigation was called, was one of the most prolific sources of litigation in Athens.

Retiring officials were attacked, not only by public-spirited citizens and individuals who had real grievances, but also by professional accusers known as sycophants, and by personal and political enemies. The sycophant hoped to profit financially by extorting "hush money." The personal enemy, assuming the guise of a public benefactor, could get revenge and the politician could embarrass a political opponent by putting him on trial, even if he did not win a verdict. When wholesale prosecutions were resorted to in such political struggles as those that centered around the Areopagus, or the revolutions of 411 and 404, a large number of them were connected with the *euthyna*.

In the fourth century, at least, the dicasts played an important rôle in legislation.[49] In the early stages of Greek history laws were drafted and presented by specially appointed legislators such as Draco and Solon. Such codes were commonly regarded as permanent. They were not to be lightly changed. The Athenian orators constantly point to the antiquity of a law as proof of its excellence. The laws of Solon, for example, were intended to endure for one hundred years.[50] The repeal of Draco's laws by Solon was exceptional. Among the Locrians, if any citizen wished to introduce a new law or change an old one he was required to present himself before the council of one thousand with a rope around his neck.[51] If he did not persuade the council, he was forthwith hanged. It is said that only one law was changed in two centuries. The Athenian constitution provided that once a year there should be a discussion in the assembly regarding the advisability of making changes in the laws. If it was voted to revise the statutes, a group of *nomothetae* selected from the dicasts heard the arguments of proposers of new laws, and of five advocates appointed to defend the law as it stood. Any citizen who desired to appear for or against the law in question was also given a hearing.

It was also the duty of the six junior archons, the *thesmothetae*, to examine the laws annually and determine whether there were any obsolete or contradictory ones. If any such were found, they were duly posted and a panel of five hundred or one thousand dicasts decided, after hearing arguments pro and con, what should be done with them. The court of *nomothetae* thus acted as a check upon hasty changes in the laws. The attitude of sworn dicasts listening to prepared arguments was different from that of a meeting of the assembly.

The process of legislation was protected by a writ known as the *graphe paranomon*,[52] or indictment for unconstitutional legislation. Anyone responsible for putting through a law without due observation of all the constitutional formalities was personally liable for one year after the passage of the law. His punishment was not fixed by law, but was determined by the jury. After the expiry of a year only, the law could be attacked or annulled. The process could also be invoked against laws or decrees that were prejudicial to the public interest. According to Aristotle,[53] the worst form of democracy is where not the law, but the multitude, is supreme and supersedes the law by its decrees. Any law or decree that contravened an existing law could be attacked and annulled in the courts. The first step in the process was to suspend the law or decree in question until a judicial decision was procured. Perhaps no process was more used in political warfare than the *graphe paranomon*. Aristophon, a contemporary of Demosthenes, is said to have boasted that he was acquitted seventy-five times on charges of making illegal motions, while Cephalus, another politician, claimed credit because he had never once been indicted, though he was the mover of more motions than any of his contemporaries.[54] Between these two extremes, it may confidently be assumed that a considerable amount of litigation, in connection with the everyday business of the assembly, originated in passing on decrees presented by this or that politician. In any slip or irregularity an opponent might find an opportunity to launch an attack. Great political duels were fought before the courts in these cases, as well as before the assembly. Where personal liability was involved, the verdict of the court might result, not only in political ruin, but also in serious financial loss in the form of a fine.

In all political systems the courts are used to collect unpaid taxes, but in Athens, owing to a peculiar feature of the system of taxation, the courts might intervene, not to collect the tax, but to determine who should pay it. Expensive public services, known as liturgies, such as the manning and maintaining of a warship for a specified time, were assigned to the wealthier citizens. If the individual selected for the task thought that a man of greater wealth had been passed over, he could take the matter to court and try to prove that the other should be required to discharge the service. This type of suit was called *antidosis*,[55] or exchange, because a complainant first challenged the proposed substitute to undertake the burden, or to exchange properties and allow the challenger to discharge it. If both proposals were rejected, the matter came before a court for adjudication.

Regular treaties were ratified by the assembly, but a special type of treaty, regulating litigation between citizens of the contracting states, could be ratified only by a court under the presidency of the *thesmothetae*.[56] The reason for this unusual procedure in connection with this class of treaty is the fact that such treaties usually provided for a special code and laid down rules of procedure for the cases that should fall under the provisions of the treaty. Under the Athenian system, as we have seen, all changes and modifications in the laws had to be approved by a panel of dicasts.

The services of the courts in administering the empire in the fifth century were very considerable, but a discussion of them belongs rather to the chapter on the administration of the empire.[57] Only one question need be raised at this point. The first assessment of the tribute was made by Aristides in 478, but it is not known just how subsequent revisions were made. It has been suggested that possibly the proposed revisions required ratification of a court, because they were like revisions of the laws. But there is no evidence for this suggestion, apart from probability. It has been further argued that remissions of the tribute were made by the assembly, but this could not be done if they had been fixed by the court.[58] In any event, the subject cities carried their appeals against the assessed tribute to the courts in Athens.

Certain features of the Athenian judicial system are directly traceable to the irresponsible independent powers possessed by each dicastery. This must be borne in mind if one would rightly judge the character of Athenian justice. There were no precedents in Athenian administration of justice, as there are in Great Britain and in the United States. Each dicastery was a law unto itself. Precedents, it is true, were cited by litigants, but their effect was psychological, not legal.

It is somewhat surprising to find that there was no provision for appeal from the verdict of a popular court. One would expect some provision for an appeal to the whole body of dicasts in certain types of cases. Plato, in the Laws,[59] recommended a court of appeal. There is no adequate explanation forthcoming for the complete abandonment of the Solonian appeal. It is well, however, to remember in this connection that appeals in English criminal cases are a recent innovation.

In modern states a pardoning power is vested in the sovereign or the president. Juries occasionally bring in a verdict of guilty with a recommendation to mercy, where there are extenuating circumstances. But in Athens there was no power superior to the people sitting in judgment in each dicastery; consequently, the dicasts must themselves take account of extenuating circumstances in reaching their verdict, and also listen to appeals for mercy, which in modern states are addressed to the authorities that exercise the pardoning power, often accompanied by popular petitions and backed by a newspaper campaign. If one keeps this situation in mind, one will understand some of the abuses that grew up in Athens and will not judge them too harshly.

Modern writers, especially lawyers, have been unsparing in their criticism of the Athenian judicial system. If one judges it by the standards of today, these strictures are largely justified. But Grote, the great historian of Greece, took a different and a fairer view. "These numerous dicasteries, inaccessible both to corruption and to intimidation, afforded the only organ which Greek politics could devise for getting redress against powerful criminals, public as well as private."

CHAPTER III

THE POLITICIANS

DEMOCRACY has been aptly described as government by discussion. This is preëminently a true description of Athenian democracy. Pericles in the Funeral Oration points out that the Athenians believed in the fullest discussion of all public questions. "The great impediment to action is, in our opinion, not discussion preparatory to action, but rather not to be instructed by debate before action."[1] Probably Pericles had in mind the attitude of the Spartans, who, according to the ephor Sthenilaidas, "did not understand the long speeches of the Athenians."

For certain purposes, the Athenian constitution required the attendance of at least six thousand in the assembly. It is obvious that such a numerous body must have been recruited from a population that lived in or near the city and the Piraeus and enjoyed considerable leisure. So it was, for the management of the empire yielded employment and emolument sufficient to maintain directly or indirectly a large percentage of the population. It was Aristides who first advised the Athenians to develop the possibilities of the league, and to quit the country and settle in the city. "He pointed out to them that all would be able to gain a living there, some by service in the army, others in the garrisons, others by taking part in public affairs." As a result of taking this advice, Aristotle calculates that "out of the proceeds of the tributes and the taxes and the contributions of the allies, more than twenty thousand persons were maintained."[2]

The great scheme of Aristides was carried out, in part at least, about the middle of the fifth century, when Pericles first realized the value of the spoils of empire. Following the advice of a political adviser to "make presents to the people from their own property," he introduced pay for the dicasts. Aristotle characterizes the measure as a bid for popular favor to counterbalance the wealth of his political rival, Cimon. The significance of this step of Pericles did not escape Athenian observers. It opened to rival politicians immense opportunities for corrupting the people. The resources of even a wealthy man like Cimon were limited; but the resources of an empire were incalculable, and available to anyone who could persuade the people to take them. This new departure evoked considerable criticism. Plato fully understood the implications of Pericles' policy. In the *Gorgias*[3] Socrates is represented as remarking, "I should like to know whether the Athenians are said to have been made better by Pericles, or, on the contrary, to have been corrupted by him; for I hear that he was the first who gave the people pay, and made them idle and cowardly, and encouraged them in the love of talk and of money."

A new situation was now created for democracy. The sovereign assembly no longer consisted mainly of the more or less homogeneous rural population of Attica, the descendants of the Marathonian heroes whom Aristophanes delighted to represent as models of civic and military virtue. There was gathered into the city a motley crowd. The Xenophontic Socrates describes them as "fullers, cobblers, builders, smiths, farmers, mechanics, merchants, and traffickers in the market-place."[4]

The development of formal rhetoric about the middle of the fifth century enabled ambitious members of the commercial and industrial classes to acquire some proficiency in the art of public speaking. Plenty of teachers, known as sophists, were ready to furnish, for a consideration, the necessary instruction, regardless of previous condition of incapacity and without interruption of business. Anyone who was able and willing to pay the price might hope to prepare himself to take a part in the discussion of public affairs. All Athenians in full possession of their political rights were permitted to speak in the assembly. People of all sorts and conditions availed themselves of the privilege. Plato[5] observes that the Athenians were ready to listen to "carpenters, smiths, shoemakers, hucksters, merchants, noble and ignoble, rich and poor" discoursing on public questions. But the number of persons who habitually spoke in the assembly was comparatively small. They were variously known as "politicians" (οἱ πολιτικοί), "speakers" (οἱ λέγοντες), "public men" (οἱ τὰ τῆς πόλεως πράττοντες). But their common and most characteristic designation was "orators" (ῥήτορες). They were the men who led the discussions and influenced public opinion as expressed in the decrees of the assembly. In a word, they were professional politicians. The designation "orators," though in no sense official, was so distinctive that it was employed even in public documents.[6] Hypereides[7] was once advocate for Euxenippus, who was impeached for not giving the best advice to the people. He argued that the defendant was not liable under the law because he did not belong to the class of orators. But this plea is not to be taken to mean that the law recognized a special class in the assembly as "orators." Hypereides was merely trying to minimize his client's responsibility for a particular action of the assembly by asserting that, since he was not a politician, he could not have appreciably influenced the decision of that body.

The orators were roughly divided into two classes. In *Demosthenes* vs. *Meidias*,[8] the plaintiff says, "Perhaps Meidias will say of me, 'He is an orator.' Well, if one who advises what he thinks is for your good without being troublesome or insistent, is an 'orator,' I would not object, or disown the name. But if an orator be what you and I know some of the speakers are, shameless fellows enriched at your expense, I would not be an orator." So also in another passage in Demosthenes,[9] orators are described either as those who plague the assembly or those who have gained the confidence of the people. And Hypereides[10] speaks of the lesser orators as mere masters of noise and tumult.

A "politician" is the nearest modern equivalent of the Athenian "orator," but the common designation of the Athenian popular leaders is "demagogue." In Greek usage, in the beginning, *demagogos* was a neutral word meaning "popular leader." Thucydides calls Cleon a "demagogue," and Isocrates applies the term to Pericles. But soon it came to have a sinister connotation, and writers using it in a good sense found it necessary to employ qualifying adjectives such as "good" or "just." Aristotle[11] definitely fixed the bad sense of the word for the modern world, as "mob leader" by defining a demagogue as a "flatterer of the people."

Among the leading orators in the assembly there was a constant struggle for leadership. The leader, who was commonly known as the *prostates*, was not official. At times it might be difficult to determine who was in the ascendant. The position of the reigning popular leader, when his leadership was acknowledged, may be compared with that of a premier, or prime minister in the British parliamentary system. His closest rival might well be compared with the unofficial leader of the opposition. But it is a mistake to press the analogy too far. There was no definite party system in Athens. Naturally men of similar aims and views tended to coöperate to achieve some definite result. For example, the attack upon the political and judicial powers of the Areopagus in the interest of democratic progress was conducted by a group of men, among whom were Ephialtes, Pericles, Archestratus, and possibly Themistocles. Ephialtes was the leader. The knights, numbering a thousand, also constituted an influential element in the assembly, as Aristophanes' appeal to them for aid against Cleon in the *Knights* shows.

Discussion of public questions, if it is to be profitable, must be guided by experts. In Athens there were always men in the assembly who, by reason of their special interests or opportunities, had gained some knowledge of particular phases of public administration. A conversation reported in the *Memorabilia* of Xenophon[12] mentions some of these topics. Socrates is represented as examining a young man as to his preparation for public life. It soon appears that he has not informed himself upon such fundamental matters as revenues, expenditures, military preparedness, the Athenian food supply, and the silver mines of Laurium. It was a favorite thesis of Plato that government cannot be administered successfully by amateurs. And sophists, like Protagoras, professed to teach their pupils "to be able to speak and act for the best in the affairs of state."[13] It is clear that the Athenians realized that on some questions they must have expert advice.

The Athenians are an understanding people, and such they are esteemed to be by the other Hellenes. Now I observe that when we are met together in the assembly, and the matter in hand relates to building, the builders are summoned as advisors; when the question is one of shipbuilding, then the shipbuilders and shipwrights; and the like of other arts. . . . And if some person offers to give them advice who is not supposed to have any skill in the art . . . they will not listen to him, but hoot and laugh at him.

The available information regarding debates in the assembly is too meager to enable us to draw any conclusions regarding the handling of special questions that involved some technical knowledge. But it may be assumed with assurance that the better class of orators, who are sometimes described as advisors, did not neglect to inform themselves on certain phases of public administration. If they were not experts in the Platonic sense, they need not be inferior to certain members of modern parliaments, who, by reason of their experience, contacts, and special interests, are looked upon as authorities when questions involving their specialties are under discussion. And the assembly gladly heard these experts. Cleon and Lycurgus, for example, were good financiers.

On occasion, matters involving the collection of information not available to the ordinary Athenian were entrusted to a special commission (συγγραφεῖς) to study and report upon them. Records of several of these commissions are available. The most important document on the subject is the report of a commission appointed to make recommendations regarding an ancient religious ceremony in which the first-fruits of the harvest were offered to the Eleusinian goddess. The ceremony had fallen into disuse, and it was intended to revive it. The work of the commission had a political, or rather imperial aspect, in that it involved the participation of the subject and allied cities of the empire. The report was adopted by the assembly in the form of a decree.[14]

The leaders of democracy in Athens were severely criticized and even reviled by their contemporaries. And modern writers, with few exceptions, have followed suit. The practice of calling them demagogues at once, so to speak, puts them on the defensive. The mere name is an accusation. "'Tis an ill business," says Bdelycleon in the *Wasps*, "to defend a maligned dog." The earliest Greek writer to give the popular leaders a "bad name" was the historian Thucydides.[15] After describing with approval the character and policy of Pericles, he says, "But the successors of Pericles, being more on an equality with each other and yet striving each to be first, were ready to surrender to the people even the conduct of public affairs to suit their whims."Aristotle[16] expresses much the same opinion: "So long as Pericles was leader of the people, things went tolerably well with the state, but when he was dead there was a great change for the worse. For the first time they chose a leader who did not belong to the upper classes." To the same effect are the tirades of Aristophanes. The degeneracy of the popular leadership is the theme of the *Knights*.[17]

> To be a Demus-leader is not now
> For lettered men nor yet for honest men,
> But for the base and ignorant.

The demagogues are always shouting their cant phrases:

> To the rabble of Athens I'll ever be true,
> I'll always battle away for the mob.

Or:

> O Demus, I'm your lover, I alone,
> Care for you, scheme for you, tend you and love you well.

In short, the demagogue is always the watchdog of the people.

It has often been said of democracies that they get just the kind of leadership they want. Aristophanes[18] is well aware of this, but one had to be cautious in speaking of democracy on the stage. "O Demus," says the chorus in the *Knights*, "you're easily led astray, you like to be flattered and deceived. Every speaker you believe, gazing with a vacant stare. Wits you have, but they're always wandering when you use your ears." Plato fully shares these views of the demagogues, but he asserts that it was Pericles who first corrupted the people. The demagogues merely followed his lead and "gave the people their own." The evils of the new democracy were not apparent in Periclean Athens, for Pericles, not the people, really ruled. "Athens," says Thucydides,[19] "though in name a democracy, was in fact ruled by her greatest citizen."

Economic conditions materially changed as the empire was organized and developed economically. The landed gentry of Attica and their peasant supporters no longer controlled the state. The merchant and small manufacturer began to make money. Political power definitely shifted to the middle classes domiciled in Athens and the Piraeus, who were engaged in industry and commerce. The new education, based upon rhetoric and easily acquired from the sophists, resident and itinerant, put into the hands of the more aggressive members of these classes the means of influencing the assembly by oratory, or the art of persuasion, as the Greeks aptly called it.

"In earlier times," says Aristotle,[20] "the demagogue was also a general, . . . but in our day, when the art of rhetoric has made such progress, orators without military experience lead the people." This generalization of Aristotle epitomizes the Athenian political situation very well. In fifth-century Athens, down to the Peloponnesian war, the generals were drawn from the best families, and from them came the most influential leaders in the assembly. Often men were elected year after year. Pericles was general for fifteen years, Nicias for fourteen years. Sometimes, like Themistocles and Aristides, one devoted himself to war and the other to the conduct of affairs.[21] It was natural that leadership should continue in the hands of men of birth and breeding, who had shown themselves interested in the fortunes of democracy even after the reform of the Areopagus. Their social background and political experience gave them an immense advantage in comparison even with the more aggressive and gifted of the middle and lower classes. Wealth, too, in the estimation of the multitude, conferred some distinction on individuals, even if they were not so liberal in its use as Cimon was. Among the leaders of democracy in this period there were men of real political and oratorical ability. Themistocles had a reputation as a speaker of parts. His oratory was a gift improved by practice. The sources of technical rhetoric were not yet available. Pericles, in the next generation, had an opportunity to profit from the newly discovered art. The meager echoes of his oratory that have survived afford but little grounds for estimating the extent of his indebtedness to rhetorical theory. But the power of his oratory is well attested. When he delivered the funeral oration over those killed in the Samian war, the women flocked about him and paid him court as if he were a victorious athlete.[22]

The rule of the generals lasted down into the Peloponnesian war. The system had its advantages. The people had a chance to elect their potential leaders every year. And out of a body of ten there was a fair chance that some would possess talents for the administration of civil affairs and the management of assemblies.

In the fourth century the union of popular leader and military leader in one and the same person became increasingly rare. War became much more of an art. A man who wished to be a general had to make war a profession. He had neither the time nor the temperament for practical politics. The citizen army had practically disappeared. The armies were composed largely of mercenaries. As a result of this separation of military and political leadership, the military enterprises of Athens languished for lack of adequate and intelligent support; and the generals got the blame.

In a well-known passage in the *Knights*,[23] presented in 424, Aristophanes satirized the new political leaders who succeeded Pericles. They may be designated the "dealer régime." According to a comic oracle, Cleon was to be ousted from his leadership by a still more disreputable rascal.

Demosthenes: The oracle says straight out
                That first there will arise a hemp *dealer*,
                Who'll be the first to manage the affairs of state.
Nicias: That's one *dealer*. What next? Go on.
Demosthenes: Next after him a second leader, a sheep *dealer*.
Nicias: That's two *dealers*. And what's to happen to him?
Demosthenes: To rule until another more detestable than he
                Shall arise. Afterwards he'll perish,
                For next comes the Paphlagonian, the leather *dealer*.

Nicias then wonders where they are to procure one more dealer to fulfill the oracle. Just then there appears a sausage-maker, the humblest of all dealers. They persuade him to proceed to oust Cleon and fulfil the oracle, which he does.

To these dealers may be added Hyperbolus the lamp dealer, and Cleophon the lyre dealer. It is not a coincidence that five popular leaders following Pericles were engaged in trade and commerce. The class from which they came was in the ascendant. These demagogues were always good speakers and sometimes men of substance. Aristophanes admits that Cleon was a powerful speaker. But he threw aside all dignity and scandalized the Pericleans by girding up his loins, striding up and down the platform, and roaring like a torrent in flood.[24] Hyperbolus[25] is said to have paid a talent for an education in the new fashion and to have practiced in the courts. The talent is doubtless an exaggeration; but at all events it is clear that Hyperbolus was a man of means. Lysicles, the drover, married Aspasia, the widow of Pericles, and was one of the generals in 429 B.C. Agyrrhius,[26] who introduced pay for attendance at the assembly, was a financier. Heracleides,[27] who increased it, was from Clazomene and was naturalized because of the high esteem in which he was held. Cleophon,[28] whose leadership fell between the revolution of the Four Hundred and the end of the war, was distinguished for his skilful financial adminis-tration year after year. One might pursue the investigation further, but enough has been said to show that these dema-gogues were not the disreputable rascals that Aristophanes represented them to be; they were not unworthy representa-tives of the class that ruled Athens in the late fifth century. The same is true of the fourth century, as had been shown by the investigations of Sundwall.[29] Out of ninety-four orators mentioned in the sources, forty-four belong to the propertied classes. Moreover, it is by no means true that only the poor-est and humblest attended the meetings of the assembly.

The successors of Pericles were not slow to find ways of winning popular favor by extensions of state pay in the form of indemnities and doles. The two-obol pay for dicasts, introduced by Pericles as a bid for popular favor, was soon (425 B.C.) raised by Cleon to three obols, that is, a half-drachma. In 410 B.C., the victory at Cyzicus restored the unity of Athens after the revolution of 411 B.C. Pay for all state services was resumed. Cleophon, a leader distinguished for his financial ability, introduced a new form of state aid. It was a two-obol dole, paid perhaps to all those who were not already in receipt of pay for state services either civil or military.[30] Shortly after the restoration of democracy in 403 B.C., Agyrrhius[31] introduced pay for attending the assembly. At first it was one obol, but soon a rival, Heracleides, raised it to two obols. Agyrrhius, not to be outdone, again raised it to three obols, the same as the pay for dicasts.

The modern method of corrupting the electorate by the appropriation of large sums for public works, which often have no justification, was practically unknown in Athens. But such buildings as the Parthenon, the Propylaea, the Odeum, and the sanctuary for the mysteries at Eleusis, begun by Pericles, furnished work and wages to many Athenians and strengthened Pericles' hold on the proletariat. The money for these splendid structures was supplied by the tribute from the subject states. The outbreak of the Peloponnesian war in 431 B.C. interrupted the building projects. To this time belongs, perhaps, the construction of the temple of Athena Nike and a part of the Erechtheum. In 409 B.C. the work on the Erechtheum was resumed under Cleophon.

The Periclean policy of expending the surplus tribute upon the adornment of Athens met with determined opposition on the part of the conservatives. They described Athens as a courtesan decked with thousand-talent temples. For the settlement of this question and others like it Athens had adopted the process of ostracism that Cleisthenes had introduced in order to enable the people by a secret ballot to protect themselves from the restoration of tyranny. But as democracy progressed, the danger of tyranny no longer threatened, and ostracism began to be used as a party weapon to decide the question of leadership between powerful rivals. There is no reason to believe that resorts to ostracism were frequent. Indeed, so cumbersome a procedure was likely to be invoked only when the struggle for leadership involved policies that aroused general public interest. So the question, whether Athens should use the tribute from the allied cities in the confederacy of Delos entirely for military preparedness against Persia, was settled by the ostracism of Thucydides in 442 B.C. He was the leader of that section of the citizens which did not favor the Periclean policy of adorning Athens with temples and other public buildings from the tribute. Henceforth, the Periclean policy prevailed. Athens protected her subject allies and expended the surplus tribute on splendid public buildings.

The last ostracism in Athens occurred in 418 B.C. The candidates for this form of exile were supposed to be Alcibiades and Nicias. Plutarch,[32] after enumerating some causes of the popular dislike of these men, adds: "To tell the simple truth, it was a struggle between the young men, who wanted war, and the elderly men, who wanted peace; one party proposed to ostracize Nicias, the other Alcibiades." But it turned out otherwise. Hyperbolus, a man of the people, expecting to prove a match in the assembly for whichever of the two should be left, had openly favored a resort to ostracism, confident that he would profit by it. But Nicias and Alcibiades united their factions and secured the ostracism of Hyperbolus. It is said that the people felt the institution had been dishonored by being used against a man like Hyperbolus, and gave it up. Plato, the comic poet, expresses this point of view when he says, "For such

as he the *ostrakon* was ne'er devised." This explanation for
the decay of ostracism need not be taken seriously. Other
more practical means of settling party disputes had been
discovered. The law of ostracism was not annulled; it
simply fell into desuetude. Even in Aristotle's day, in the
late fourth century, the question of ostracism still appeared
on the agenda of the assembly annually on the sixth
prytany, but was never taken up.

In addition to the annual elections for generals and occasional ostracisms, litigation furnished a variety of ways of
attacking politicians. Litigation often had a twofold effect.
It might eliminate one leader and elevate another. All
Athenian officials, including military officers, had to submit to a *euthyna* or audit, at the end of the official year. At
the *euthyna* any charge affecting official conduct could be
brought against the retiring official. Against the generals,
misappropriation of funds voted for a campaign or collected from the subordinate cities in the way of tribute, was
the usual charge. Sometimes personal wrongdoing constituted the charge. For example, Paches, the conqueror of
Mytilene in 427 B.C., is said to have committed suicide in
court because two women of Mytilene appeared to charge
him with procuring the death of their husbands, that he
might the more securely force his attentions upon them.[33]
An ambitious beginner in politics might win his way to
popularity by prosecuting a retiring general at his audit.
Pericles first came into prominence by prosecuting Cimon
for accepting a bribe in the campaign against the island of
Thasos in 464-3 B.C. Even if a political leader was not a
general, he might be elected as the member of an embassy,
and be under the obligation of giving an account of his part
in the negotiations, or of answering charges of bribery.
Thus Demosthenes prosecuted his rival Aeschines for
treasonable practices on the embassy that preceded the
peace of Philocrates in 346 B.C. The speeches of both

Demosthenes and Aeschines are extant, and are veritable mines of information regarding current events. Normally, embassies of the fifth century were comparatively simple affairs, with little or no chance for corrupt practices. It was not until the struggle with Philip began, that money was freely used for the purpose of bribing the representatives and leaders of the Greek states.

The lot, used so widely in Athens, fell upon all alike. An active politician might very well be selected for an office and be exposed to attacks at his audit. Thus Aeschines, in his attack upon Ctesiphon for proposing a crown for Demosthenes, urged the objection that, when the proposed crown should be conferred on Demosthenes, he would still be subject to audit in connection with two minor offices he held. According to law, no official could be crowned or otherwise honored until he had passed his audit.

In Athens there were no public prosecutors. But there were plenty of professional accusers, known as "sycophants," who made a business of prosecuting or threatening to prosecute, often with little regard to the justness of their charges. In spite of laws tending to curb their pernicious activities, the sycophants drove a thriving and remunerative business, chiefly as blackmailers.[34] Their procedure was to threaten a man with criminal proceedings, and then arrange for the payment of "hush money." There are plenty of indications that the services of these professional accusers were used by quite reputable and prominent public men, to harass and discredit their opponents. Even Demosthenes did not scruple to write speeches for delivery, by others, against his political opponents.[35] These relationships are not easy to prove, for the sycophant was always ready with plausible personal reasons why he prosecuted a defendant. The prosecutors of Androtion, Timocrates, and Aristocrates are examples. Demosthenes wrote the speeches to be delivered by political henchmen. A favorite trick was to charge a politician with some infraction of military law, such as failing to answer the call to arms, desertion, abandoning arms, etc. There was no statute of limitations for these offenses. After a lapse of time such a charge might be hard to disprove. In any event, any suspicion of dereliction from military duty was harmful to a politician's popularity and prestige.

Unfounded charges of homicide against politicians are not unknown. It was a most effective weapon in political litigation, because the accused was excluded from any public assembly until he was acquitted. He would be obliged, for example, to withdraw from any prosecutions in which he was engaged. He was regarded as polluted until he was acquitted. A client of Antiphon, the first of the Attic orators, tells a plausible story of how he was prevented from carrying on a case against some officials for defrauding the public treasury by a charge of homicide. It appears that, as choregus in charge of the collecting and training of a group of boys for choral competition with other tribes, he was charged with responsibility for the death of one of the boys, to whom the musical director had given some medicine for throat trouble.[36]

Besides the sycophant, politicians could rely on the aid of the clubs, to which they commonly belonged. These clubs were, in many cases, devoted to forwarding the interests of their members in politics and litigation, as Thucydides tells us. It is obvious that a group of men more or less actively interested in public life could be of real service to one another. Grote,[37] with his marvelous insight into things Athenian, has admirably described these clubs as existing "partly for purposes of amusement, but chiefly pledging the members to stand by each other in objects of political ambition, in judicial trials, in accusation or defense of official men after the period of office had expired, in carrying points through the assembly, etc." Not all the activities of these clubs were beyond reproach, such as the suppression of evidence by terrorizing witnesses, the pressure put upon an accuser to desist, and even, in the fifth century, the corruption of jurors. But there were plenty of legitimate ways of lending assistance that were open to the friends of a litigant, such as advancing money, procuring witnesses, acting as advocates, discovering the accuser's proposed method of attack, the influencing of public opinion in favor of the accused, and entering counter-suits. As litigation in democratic Athens was closely associated with politics, these methods were available in political prosecutions, as well as in elections, and in carrying proposals in the assembly.

One would expect that the clubs would surely use their influence in a vote of ostracism, but there is no mention of club activities until the struggle between Alcibiades and Nicias in 418-17 B.C. But this need occasion no surprise, for details concerning the earlier ostracisms are wholly lacking. The casual manner in which Plutarch refers to the activity of the club of Phaeax as being active in securing the ostracism of Hyperbolus would seem to indicate that the clubs were generally active in ostracism. The most spectacular political activity of the clubs was in the revolution of 411 B.C., when Peisander, one of the oligarchic conspirators, organized the clubs to overthrow the democracy in a constitutional manner. They were responsible for the propaganda in favor of a liberal oligarchy as well as for the tenor, if not the wording, of speeches made in the assembly. Similarly, in the oligarchy of the Thirty the reactionary elements were centered in the clubs under the control of a central committee of five, known as the ephors, in imitation of the Spartan magistrates so named.[38]

A democracy of the kind developed at Athens was necessarily managed by decrees expressing the people's will on matters not taken care of by some specific law. Where all officials were subordinated to the assembly, it could not be otherwise. As a consequence, a leading politician was identified with a great many decrees and laws in the course of his public career. Great care was taken that there should be no infringement of the constitution in the passing of decrees or the enactment of laws. To this end the mover was held personally responsible for any infringement of the constitutional rules. It was no defense that the members of the assembly had voted for the law or the resolution.

The indictment for illegal legislation originated in the fifth century, when the Areopagus was stripped of its political powers, including the supervision of laws and the duty of seeing that the magistrates enforced them, but there is little mention of its use. This situation led Mahaffy[39] to put forward the theory that so long as ostracism was used there was little recourse to the *graphe paranomon*. This is an attractive suggestion. There are few instances of the use of the procedure in the fifth century,[40] but it was esteemed important enough by the revolutionists of 411 B.C. to be suspended, so that they might have a free hand to deal with the constitution as they saw fit. According to Thucydides,[41] the only recommendation of a constitution commission appointed at that time was to suspend the *graphe paranomon* and all forms of legal action, against any proposal that might be made in the assembly. This action shows clearly that the committee regarded the *graphe paranomon* as an important constitutional safeguard. However, Mahaffy's theory is supported by the enormous number of prosecutions that were launched in the fourth century, which are not to be entirely accounted for by the great abundance of source material for the fourth as compared with the fifth century. The struggle with Macedonia imported much bitterness into Athenian domestic politics, as is evidenced by all sorts of what may be called political prosecutions, including indictments for illegal or

unsuitable legislation. Some notion of the prevalence of
the *graphe paranomon* may be had from the fact that
Aristophon, a politician contemporary with Demosthenes,
boasted that he had been indicted seventy times under
the statute.

In the political struggles between the adherents of democracy and its enemies, litigation was sometimes used wholesale. The way for restricting the power of the Areopagus
was prepared by a series of prosecutions of individual
members with a view to lessening the prestige of that
ancient and honorable body. Similarly, the oligarchic revolutions of 411 and 404 were facilitated by the prosecution
of a number of democratic officials and politicians in order
to discredit the system, if possible.[42]

While the leadership in the assembly was usually in the
hands of one man, such as Pericles or Cleon, the leader
always had about him others whose services were available
for putting through decrees, defending policies, prosecuting
politicians and retiring officials, and generally making
themselves useful to the leader. Plutarch remarks that
Pericles, knowing that familiarity may breed contempt,
"did not address the people on every occasion, but kept
himself for emergencies. The rest of his policy he carried
out by commissioning his friends and other public speakers."
Demosthenes also had friends and allies to whom he could
entrust certain tasks commensurate with their ability.

But the possession of a group of political friends, allies,
and assistants involved some liability to them. Opponents
who did not feel themselves strong enough to attack the
leader openly, would prosecute his lieutenants in the courts.
Thus the great oration *On the Crown* was not delivered in
defense of Demosthenes himself but in behalf of Ctesiphon,
who was prosecuted for carrying a measure to confer a
crown on Demosthenes as a reward for his long public
service. The opponents of Demosthenes could not let this

honor go unchallenged, as it involved an expression of public approval of his whole administration. Failing to defeat the measure in the assembly, they raised technical objections and prosecuted Ctesiphon as the mover. The resulting trial was not in effect different from a debate in the assembly. The verdict of the five hundred jurors in the case was really a vote of confidence in Demosthenes and his policies.

Sometimes friends of a politician who were of little or no political significance were attacked in the courts merely to annoy and embarrass him.[43] Thus Aspasia was accused of an offense which may be described in modern legal language as "contributing to the delinquency of free women." Pericles appeared in her defense and begged her off, shedding copious tears at the trial. His friend Anaxagoras was also attacked. "Diopeithes," Plutarch tells us, "brought in a bill providing for the public impeachment of such as did not believe in the gods, or who taught doctrines regarding the heavens, directing suspicion against Pericles." Pericles defended Anaxagoras. He was condemned, but managed, possibly with the aid of Pericles, to escape to Lampsacus. Another friend of Pericles, Pheidias the sculptor, was accused of embezzlement in connection with his work on the Acropolis sculptures. That the purpose of all these attacks was to humiliate and discredit Pericles is shown by the fact that soon afterwards a charge of malversation of public funds was brought against him. The case was tried by a jury of fifteen hundred instead of the usual five hundred. Pericles was convicted and fined. This happened in July, 430 B.C. The war was in progress and he alone really had the public confidence. Presently he was reëlected general.

The possibilities of litigation as a weapon in the hands of one's political opponents is well set forth by Demosthenes:[44]

Afterwards when those who were bent on doing me mischief conspired and brought indictments, audits, impeachments, and the rest of it against me, not at first in their own persons, but in such names as they imagined would most effectually screen themselves (for you surely know and remember that every day of that first period I was arraigned, and that neither the desperation of Sosicles, nor the malignity of Philocrates, nor the madness of Diondas and Melantus, nor anything else was left untried by them against me), on all those occasions chiefly through the gods, secondly through you I was preserved. . . . On the impeachments, when you acquitted me and did not give the prosecutors a fifth part of the votes, you pronounced that my policy was best; by my acquittal on the indictments my motions and counsels were shown to be legal, by your passage of my accounts you acknowledged my whole conduct to have been honest and incorruptible.

Demosthenes, it will be observed, regarded a favorable verdict of the court as public approval for his policies. In this he was right. The jury of five hundred that sat on each case was a cross-section of the Athenian people and represented, as no modern court can, the prevailing public opinion quite as well as the vote of a modern parliament on a want of confidence motion, or a popular election.

CHAPTER IV

FREEDOM OF SPEECH

ORATORY had always played an important rôle in Greece. In the Homeric Age doughty deeds and wise counsel distinguished the chief leaders. Achilles is characterized in the *Iliad* as a speaker of words and a doer of deeds. Into his mouth Homer has put the noblest speech in the poem. The political organization of the Homeric state was an aristocratic monarchy. At the head was a king supported by a council of the lesser chiefs, whom he constantly consulted on all important matters of state. There was an assembly consisting of all free men, which met irregularly to hear the decisions and proposals of the royal council, presented by the king or a member of the council. In a society thus organized oratory was essentially aristocratic. There was not complete freedom of speech. Only chiefs could address the royal council; but no man was denied the right to speak in the assembly, though it was always assumed that no member of the lower classes possessed the gift of eloquence.

An incident described in the second book of the *Iliad* (212-14) illustrates this point of view. At an assembly of the Greek soldiers in the camp before Troy, Thersites, a common soldier, undertook to criticize the chieftains. The poet, voicing the sentiments of the aristocratic society, represents Thersites as a poor speaker. "Only Thersites chattered on, the uncontrolled of speech, whose mind was full of words many and disorderly, wherewith to strive against the chiefs idly and in no good order."

In Athens freedom of speech was one of the cornerstones of democracy. Appreciation and praise of it constitute a commonplace in the literature. Freedom of speech is the prerogative of the free man.

> That is the slave's lot, not to speak one's thought.[1]

The unhappy Phaedra, in the *Hippolytus* of Euripides (421 ff.), voices her hopes for her sons as follows:

> But free with tongues
> Unfettered, flourish they, their home yon burg
> Of glorious Athens.

And Ion,[2] in the play that bears his name, still ignorant of his mother's identity, prays:

> Of Athens' daughters may my mother be
> That by my mother may free speech be mine.

Full political rights and freedom of speech for all are the distinctive characteristics of democracy. And Athens had the reputation of enjoying the greatest liberty of speech in all Greece.[3] An aristocratic critic[4] of Athenian democracy in the late fifth century, when it was still triumphantly successful, both at home and abroad, explains why complete equality in public speech was a vital element of democracy as it was conceived in Athens:

The poorer classes and the people there are justly entitled to have the predominance over the well-born and the rich on this ground, that it is the people which mans the ships and gives the city its power, and that it is the steersmen, boatswains, lieutenants, lookout men, and shipwrights who make the city powerful rather than the heavy-armed hoplites and the men of birth and character. This being so, it seems just that the whole body of citizens should share in office, and that those of the citizens who wish to speak should have it in their power.

Freedom of speech for all, according to this shrewd and cynical aristocrat, is not only just, but also expedient, as he proceeds to point out.

Someone might say that they ought not to have allowed anyone to take his turn in speaking and giving counsel, but only the most capable and best; but here again they determine very rightly in allowing the unworthy also to speak. For if it were men of character who spoke and deliberated, the result would be good for those resembling themselves, but not good for the democracy. As it is, a worthless man who so wishes gets up and speaks and attains what is good for himself and for those like him. It might be said: How would such a man know what was good for himself or the people? But the people realize that his ignorance and rascality and friendship towards themselves are more profitable than the virtue and wisdom and hostility of the honourable man. The best kind of city would not then result from such practices, but the democratic constitution would in that way be best preserved.

This opinion must not be dismissed as a bit of irony. Rather it has the merit of being entirely honest. This aristocrat frankly admits that under an aristocracy

the good will hold the bad in check and will not allow madmen to advise or speak or sit in the assembly. As a result, then, of these excellent conditions, the democracy would soon fall into slavery.

In theory, every Athenian citizen possessed the right of speaking in the assembly. Readers of Aristophanes and other Greek writers not favorable to extreme democracy, get the impression that the right of free speech was shamefully abused by those who were ambitious to win political influence. In a measure this is true. The Athenian assembly differed from modern governing bodies in that, unlike representative bodies, it was responsible to no one. The sole restriction upon the power of the assembly was the rule that its decrees must not contravene the constitution. Whether any particular decree was in fact *ultra vires* was determined by a court at the behest of any citizen who wished to challenge the action of the assembly and file a *graphe paranomon*.

In modern times various checks have been put upon the exercise of political power by the people. The representative system introduces the element of responsibility into popular governing bodies, and second chambers interpose delays. In modern times the constitutional checks apply to the whole body in the exercise of its political functions; in Athens the safeguards applied to individuals. In one way or another all public speakers in the assembly could theoretically be held responsible for their advice and their promises, but in practice the matter was not so simple. Restrictions were put both upon the persons entitled to freedom of speech and upon what could be said by those entitled to the privilege. Any person found guilty of certain offenses was deprived of the right of public speech in the council, the assembly, or the courts. License in speech ($\pi\alpha\rho\rho\eta\sigma\iota\alpha$) as distinguished from freedom of speech ($\iota\sigma\eta\gamma\rho\iota\alpha$) was checked by libel laws, the first of which was included in the legislation of Solon.

By extending to the lower classes the right to sit in the assembly and by permitting any one to prosecute a wrongdoer, Solon materially increased the number of those entitled to speak. His reforms depended for success upon the fullest coöperation of all classes in the citizen body. Any measure that would remove possible causes of friction would be helpful. The law forbade slanderous statements regarding the dead under any circumstances, and regarding the living "in temples, courts of law, public offices, and during festivals." The penalty was three drachmas payable to the plaintiff and two drachmas to the public treasury. This sum was not large enough to cause financial embarrassment or to arouse personal bitterness.[5] In the *Laws*,[6] Plato proposed to punish all slanderous and abusive language without exception. "Concerning abuse there shall be this one law to cover all cases. No one shall abuse anyone." A general libel law is found in the legislation of Zaleucus.[7]

As democracy progressed, Solon's law was revised. Instead of the definition of libel as "speaking evil," there was substituted a list of actionable words. The words mentioned by Lysias[8] are "murderer, abuser of father or mother, and thrower-away of a shield," but the list does not purport to be exhaustive. The penalty under the revised law was markedly higher, five hundred drachmas divided proportionately, as in Solon's law, between the plaintiff and the public treasury.

Magistrates in their official capacity were specially protected against slander.[9] The penalty was disfranchisement. The magistrate could himself inflict a summary fine upon anyone who spoke disrespectfully of his official acts in a public office. The truth of an alleged slanderous or libelous statement was a defense, with one exception. A law forbade anyone to reproach a man or woman with engaging in trade in the market place.[10] In this case the truth could be no defense. Indeed, the greater the truth the greater the libel.

One admirable feature of a libel suit was the fact that it was subject to arbitration.[11] The parties were brought face to face and an opportunity for retraction and forgiveness was afforded before they embarked upon a lawsuit with all its possibilities of personal bitterness.

It is not possible to date the revised law of libel. The section of the law guarding from reproach those engaged in trade might belong to any period, but one inevitably thinks of it as a measure of the restored democracy in 403 B.C. Such a law would suit the time when the butcher, the baker, and the candlestick-maker finally came to their own politically.

The Solonian law specifically forbade slander in the courts. If this prohibition appeared in the revised laws it did not apply to the principals in a case, as witness the abusive exchanges between Demosthenes and Aeschines. According to Demosthenes,[12] audiences enjoyed these exhibitions. Witnesses, however, were accorded protection; actionable words could not be applied to them. Among the speeches of Lysias[13] is one delivered in an action for defamation of a witness. The salient facts are as follows: A young Athenian named Theomnestus, in the course of a prosecution in which he was the defendant, had said that one of the witnesses against him had killed his own father. Afterwards the witness sued Theomnestus for libel and secured the services of Lysias as his lawyer. The line of defense adopted by Theomnestus is interesting. He admitted having said that the plaintiff "had killed his father," but claimed that the words were not actionable. The actionable word in the law was "murderer," which he had on no occasion applied to the plaintiff. Such a defense may seem preposterous, and one would expect an Athenian court to reject it at once. Like the modern layman, the Athenian dicast was suspicious of technicalities. The final outcome of the trial is not known, but it is possible that the arbitrator decided in favor of Theomnestus' contention and that the plaintiff was responsible for the appeal to the court. In favor of this view it may be pointed out that the plaintiff might have been expected to refer to the arbitrator's decision if it was favorable to him. Moreover, one is surprised at the absurdity of Theomnestus' contention, if he had not some reason to expect that it might find favor in the eyes of others. Ample grounds for such an expectation would have been furnished by the arbitrator's verdict in favor of Theomnestus. But these considerations are not decisive.

There is some difference of opinion whether the revised law, listing actionable words, was intended to clarify the Solonian law by defining slander, or whether it made certain statements slanderous no matter when or where they were uttered,[14] still leaving it possible for a court to punish under the Solonian law any statement it deemed slanderous which was uttered in temples, law courts, public offices, or during festivals. The raising of the fine for uttering actionable words to five hundred drachmas instead of the five drachmas in the Solonian law for "speaking ill" (κακῶς λέγειν) seems to point to a fundamental revision of the law of libel. The Theomnestus case shows that in a court only actionable words constituted libel. Otherwise, the plaintiff would not have argued that to say a man "killed his father" is equivalent to calling him a "murderer." Under the Solonian law, as reported by Plutarch, the statement which Theomnestus admitted he made in court was unquestionably libelous (κακῶς λέγειν). All the plaintiff would have been required to do was to prove that it was false. There is the possibility that the plaintiff chose to bring the libelous words within the list of actionable words in order to secure the infliction of the higher penalty, five hundred drachmas. But such a procedure does not fit in with the plaintiff's virtual apology for suing for libel at all. On the whole it seems more likely that the words which could be construed as libelous were limited to a specific group known as "actionable words." Such a law would not interfere with a litigant's undoubted right to discredit an opposing witness. Charges affecting the character and integrity of a witness were, if true, always susceptible of proof. In the Theomnestus case, if the witness had indeed been responsible for his father's death, evidence to that effect could have been introduced. On the other hand, the litigant's right to discredit witnesses would have been seriously curtailed if he were required to prove every sort of statement about a witness that might be construed as "ill speaking" under the broad Solonian law.

Libel laws did not interfere with freedom of speech in the Athenian popular assembly. Neither were amenities of debate preserved, as they are in modern representative bodies by the requirement that the language be parliamentary. If a speaker respected the dead and avoided actionable words, he could indulge in the widest range of personality and invective without danger of outraging public opinion. That the Greek attitude toward the use of abusive language in public is quite different from ours[15] may be seen in the assembly described in the first book of the *Iliad*, where Achilles and Agamemnon exchange the most insulting epithets. In Athens actions for libel were viewed with disfavor. The plaintiff in such suits was regarded as mean and litigious. The victim of abusive language was apparently expected to reply in kind, and usually he was both able and willing to do so.

According to a law of Solon, dealing with the procedure of the assembly, the herald asked, "Who of those above fifty years of age desires to address the assembly?"[16]After all these had spoken, the herald then invited the younger men to speak. But Aeschines laments that in his day this excellent law was no longer observed. The herald simply asked, "Who wishes to speak?" This formula appears regularly in Aristophanes.[17] Hence we may infer that the age qualification was obsolete in the late fifth century. But there was always a prejudice against youthful speakers in the assembly. So general was this prejudice that handbooks on rhetoric suggest to the young speaker the advisability of anticipating this feeling on the part of his hearers and seeking to propitiate them.[18] Plutarch has recorded a neat repartee of a youthful orator. Demades, a contemporary of Demosthenes, had proposed divine honors for Alexander. Pytheas, a young man, opposed the measure. When some one asked him, "How do you, at your age, venture to talk about such important measures?" Pytheas replied, "Well, Alexander, whom you propose to make a god, is younger than I am."[19]

It is no easy matter to address several thousand people in the open air, even when they are orderly and attentive, but if, like the Athenian assembly, they were always volubly critical and often unruly and tumultuous, the difficulty was materially increased. There was always some provision made for keeping at least a semblance of order in the assembly, by ejecting individual interrupters, but when a part of the audience wished to express its disapproval to the point of silencing a speaker, there was no recourse.

In his *Memorabilia*, Xenophon[20] tells how the youthful Glaucon was dragged from the platform and became a laughing stock when he insisted upon trying to address the assembly. But the audience was not entirely without justification. It appears that he had taken no pains to inform himself upon the normal subjects of discussion in the assembly. Demosthenes' first attempts to address the assembly were utter failures, though he had taken great pains to perfect himself in rhetoric and public speaking, as Plutarch[21] tells us. He had been successful in getting judgment against Aphobus, one of his guardians, whom he charged with embezzlement. Owing to his success in forensic oratory, he turned his attention to the assembly. "But he was interrupted by their clamors and laughed at for his inexperience. In addition to a weak voice and indistinct utterance, he indulged in long periods and abnormal figures of speech." If the account of Plutarch is true, it is an interesting commentary on the essential fairness of Athenian audiences. In the dicastery they patiently listened to him and gave him justice when his private interest was at stake, but when he undertook to discuss matters of public concern they lost patience with his weak voice and confused periods. The refusal to listen involved no material loss to Demosthenes.

There are a good many indications that the assembly was intolerant and suspicious of speakers who were thought to be disloyal to democracy.[22] This is exactly what we should expect in a country like Greece, where there was constant oscillation between oligarchy and democracy. But a more serious charge of interference with the free expression of opinions that did not meet with the approval of the majority, is often made by contemporary critics of Athenian democracy. "I know," says Isocrates,[23] "that it is hazardous to oppose your views, and that though this is a free government, there exists no freedom of speech in this assembly except that which is enjoyed by the most reckless orators who care nothing for your welfare." And Plato[24] represents Socrates as excusing his own failure to take part in public life by saying that no man can safely oppose the populace either in Athens or elsewhere and try to prevent lawless and unjust things from being done in the state. In confirmation of these animadversions one might cite the conduct of the assembly in the trial of the generals, when those who appealed to constitutional safeguards were silenced with threats of violence. But this was an unusual situation and should be used with caution.

There are indications that members of the assembly were not always intolerant of unfavorable criticism. They listened to reproofs from Pericles, who was an aristocrat and an Alcmaeonid. It is true that no one doubted his patriotism and his loyalty to democracy. But they listened also to Alcibiades, another scion of the Alcmaeonid family, and forgave him even after he betrayed them. One suspects that he did not entirely conceal in Athens the contempt for democracy which he so freely expressed in Sparta[25] when he was in exile.

The Athenians were jealous and suspicious of their politicians and were distrustful of their own susceptibility to the influences of oratory. Meetings of the assembly were always opened by the pronouncement of a solemn curse against those who by speech should deceive the assembly, the council, or the *heliaea*. The use of the term *heliaea*, the ancient designation for the popular court, instead of the later *dicasterion*, shows that the practice is very old and antedates the introduction of dicasteries under Cleisthenes.

When, under the Cleisthenian régime, the assembly gained the right to try any public offenders, this power was chiefly used to punish men who abused the confidence of the people. The earliest example of the exercise of this right is the trial of Miltiades,[26] the victor at Marathon. The general charge against him was "wrongdoing" (ἀδικία), but the specific form of wrongdoing was deceiving the people by the promises he rashly made in connection with an unsuccessful expedition to Paros. The penalty of death was proposed, and but for the intervention of the *prytaneis*, the committee that presided in the assembly, it would have been voted. As it was, a fine of fifty talents was inflicted. This experience may have suggested the advisability of seeking protection against popular leaders who abused their influence, by a law directed against those who deceived the people.

Demosthenes[27] mentions an old law which provided severe punishment for anyone who, by promises, deceived the people, the council, or the dicastery. If Demosthenes is quoting accurately, the appearance of the word "dicastery" instead of *heliaea* shows that the law was not earlier than the reforms of Cleisthenes.[28]

So important did it seem to the Athenians to keep a check on those who abused their confidence, that they devised a constitutional arrangement for ensuring at stated intervals a popular consideration of the matter. Once a year, in the sixth prytany, it was mandatory upon the *prytaneis* to make provision in the program for "presenting" the names of those "who had made promises to the people and had not performed them."[29] Names could be presented at any meeting. But the requirement that the subject should be made an order of business once a year did not allow the people to forget so vital a matter. Legally, a vote of the people against any individual thus presented carried no penalty. It lay with the prosecutor to decide whether the case should be dropped or brought to trial before a regular court. But a vote against a man in the assembly must have been very prejudicial to his interests in any subsequent criminal proceedings. Indictments by a grand jury in our own practice, and the virtual trial of alleged criminals by the press in sensational cases, are not really different, so far as the interests of the accused are concerned. In both cases there is a likelihood that the prospective jurors or dicasts have been influenced. No system of popular justice can escape this danger. In favor of the Athenian system it may be pointed out that the Athenian alleged wrongdoer "presented" to the assembly had at least an opportunity to defend himself. But no man can adequately defend himself against a newspaper campaign.

"Deceiving the people" is such a vague and general charge that it must have been difficult to substantiate it in a court of law. Few cases could be as simple as that of Miltiades, in which a military disaster was sufficient proof for the assembly, sitting as a court, that Miltiades had deceived them. The only other certain early example of legal proceedings against deceivers of the people is the action taken against those who were regarded as responsible for the condemnation of the generals for failing to pick up the dead and the shipwrecked sailors after the naval battle of Arginusae in 406 B.C. So far as we can judge, the trial resulted in a flagrant miscarriage of justice. No opportunity was afforded the generals for an adequate defense. Apart from their written official report to the council, they were permitted to make a brief statement before the assembly. Some hostile members of the assembly, sensing a favorable attitude on the part of the people,[30] on the plea that it was too late to take a vote, moved an adjournment. The council was instructed to bring in a bill providing for the disposal of the case. At a subsequent meeting a motion was passed. It provided that, since the people had heard the generals in their own defense at the previous assembly, they should at once vote by tribes on the question of the guilt of all. All constitutional efforts made to stop the motion failed, and the generals were condemned *en bloc*.

There was soon a revulsion of popular feeling, and steps were taken to punish those responsible for inflaming the people.

And not long afterwards [says Xenophon] the Athenians repented, and they voted that "presentments" [in the assembly] be brought against any who had deceived the people, that they furnish bondsmen until such time as they should be brought to trial, and that Callixenus [the man who had made the motion providing for the trial of the generals] be included among them. Presentments were brought against four others also and they were put into confinement by their bondsmen. But when there broke out afterwards a factional dispute (civil discord), these men escaped before being brought to trial.[31]

Upon the overthrow of the Thirty and the restoration of democracy, Callixenus returned under the general amnesty but was hated by everybody and died of starvation.

According to Diogenes Laertius[32] there was a popular reaction against the condemnation and execution of Socrates, though there was no irregularity in the conduct of the case. One of his accusers, Meletus, was condemned to death and the other two, Anytus and Lycon, were exiled. The source of this account is unknown. There is no mention of such a trial in contemporary accounts. It is to be expected that Xenophon would have mentioned it in the chapters of the *Memorabilia* which are devoted especially to a defense of Socrates against the accusations of the prosecutors. If there was such a trial the indictment must have charged them with deceiving the people.

In Athens the task of prosecuting criminals was the privilege of any citizen. It mattered not whether his motives were the public weal or personal revenge. Volunteer prosecutors who were unfair and unscrupulous were known as "sycophants."Among the means "devised for correcting this abuse" was the provision for "presenting" sycophants also to the assembly.[33] They had deceived the people by deceiving a dicastery, a representative public body.

An orator suspected of not giving the best advice to the people could be impeached in the assembly. The reason was that he was suspected of receiving bribes from the enemy. This feature puts the offense of the orator in the same class as betrayal of military posts or subversion of the government.

Among the orators impeached on this ground is Callistratus.[34] He was associated with the institution of the second Athenian confederacy in 378-7 B.C. The circumstances of the charge are not known. Philocrates, the negotiator of the peace that bears his name (346 B.C.), was impeached by Hypereides for taking money to support the Macedonian cause. The indictment charged the acceptance of money from the enemies of Athens.[35] Demosthenes tells of a threat by Aeschines to impeach him. He does not mention the charge, but it has been conjectured that it was the commendation of bad measures to the assembly.[36] These instances are sufficient to show that only prominent orators were impeached for giving bad advice. And since it is virtually a prosecution for accepting bribes, it could not very well be otherwise; for no one would think of bribing any but those known to have a considerable influence on public policy.

The *graphe paranomon*,[37] used to test the validity of legislative acts of the assembly, was in principle a prosecution for deceiving the people. The form of the action—*graphe*, not *dike*—shows that the punishment of the mover was the real purpose of the action. His conviction *ipso facto* invalidated the law. There was a statute of limitations. After the expiration of a year the mover could not be punished, but it was permitted to prosecute him in order to invalidate the law by court action. It is illogical to prosecute a man who in the eyes of the law has committed no crime and cannot be punished. But it was a simple way of getting the issue before the court. Besides, the mover suffered some discredit if the legislation he sponsored was declared unconstitutional or inexpedient. The *graphe paranomon* was thus a check upon the abuse of freedom of speech in the assembly.

The loss of the right of free speech was often due to a man's failure to discharge his financial obligations to the treasury, or was a punishment for crime. Complete disfranchisement or *atimia*[38] was a severe punishment even when a man was allowed to retain his property. The privileges of citizenship in the ancient world were highly prized. One who suffered disfranchisement became practically a political and social outcast. He was excluded from courts and assemblies. This means that he lost, among other privileges, the right to speak in public, either as an orator, or as a litigant, or as a witness. Partial *atimia* took various forms. Among them was the loss of the right to speak in the assembly, or the right to bring a criminal action in the courts.

The result of this type of punishment was that certain classes of criminals lost the right to advise their fellow-citizens in the council or the assembly, or to represent them as volunteer public prosecutors. Furthermore, *atimia*, when inflicted by verdict of a court, was lifelong. There was no pardon or parole except in times of national danger when a general amnesty restored full rights of citizenship. But amnesties were of infrequent occurrence.

The Athenian system provided still another means of depriving unworthy citizens of the right to speak in the assembly. It was known as a scrutiny (δοκιμασία) of orators.[39] If one of the habitual speakers in the assembly was suspected of certain specified dishonorable acts, he could be prosecuted, not for the offense, but for continuing to speak in the assembly after committing the offense. The penalty was disqualification.

If the convicted person continued to speak in the assembly, he was, like other convicted criminals, liable to summary arrest and punishment. The *dokimasia* of orators was concerned only with the criminal and dishonorable acts that had not already been made the basis of a criminal prosecution. The acts mentioned in *Aeschines* vs. *Timarchus*, the leading case of *dokimasia* of orators, fall into four classes; (1) offenses against parents, (2) military offenses, (3) the prostitution of one's body, (4) the disgraceful squandering of one's patrimony. The offenses in the first three categories were indictable and could be punished in the regular way. But squandering patrimony furnished no ground for an indictment. It is to be observed that where a choice lay between *dokimasia* and a normal criminal prosecution, the *dokimasia* carried a lighter penalty.

The procedure was unusual. The process was initiated in the assembly by a formal summons (ἐπαγγελλία) to the orator to appear before a court for trial. The purpose of this rather dramatic procedure was to remind the community of the fact that unworthy persons were not permitted to address and advise their fellow-citizens. Furthermore, the accused was caught, so to speak, *in flagrante delicto*. Two cases of *dokimasia* of orators are known. Aeschines successfully prosecuted Timarchus for prostituting his person and squandering his patrimony. The purpose was to prevent Timarchus from participating with Demosthenes in the prosecution of Aeschines for treason on an embassy to Macedonia. It would seem that the process was not often used, for Timarchus had long been active in political life. According to one source, he had introduced more than one measure into the assembly.[40] It is to the rarity of this type of prosecution, in all probability, that Demosthenes is referring in his speech *On the Embassy* when he says of Aeschines, "You can't claim that owing to inexperience you have nothing to say. You who conduct novel prosecutions like dramas, and win them too, without witnesses." The difficulty of proving such charges as Aeschines made against Timarchus is manifest. Aeschines was well aware of it, and took pains to show that it was unreasonable to expect proof of scandalous conduct when the only possible witnesses were men who would refuse to compromise themselves by admitting that they were participants. .Aeschines did succeed in winning a verdict, much to the surprise of others as well as Demosthenes.

In a speech of Lysias there is a reference to another case of *dokimasia* of orators, which has not been noticed as it deserves. About 384 B.C., Lysistheus denounced Theomnestus for speaking in the assembly when he was disqualified because he had thrown away his shield. The defendant gained public sympathy and was acquitted, probably because the alleged offense had been committed ten years before.[41] The Timarchus case was tried before a dicastery presided over by the *thesmothetae*, but the Theomnestus case came before the assembly itself. The charge was for "speaking in the assembly when he had no right to do so because he had abandoned his arms." He had not been convicted of abandonment of arms, because an effort was made to prove that charge by means of witnesses who were afterwards prosecuted by Theomnestus for perjury.[42] The success of the prosecution turned on the proof that he had thrown away his arms, just as, in the case of Timarchus, Aeschines had to prove the charges of disgraceful conduct on the part of Timarchus. The difficulty in classifying the case as a *dokimasia* lies in the fact that it was tried in the assembly, while the law as cited by Aeschines[43] specified that such cases should be tried in a law court.

The technical terms "summons" ($\epsilon\pi\alpha\gamma\gamma\epsilon\lambda\lambda\iota\alpha$) and "scrutiny" ($\delta o\kappa\iota\mu\alpha\sigma\iota\alpha$), which are mentioned in the law, occur nowhere in the speech of Lysias against Theomnestus. But these objections need occasion no difficulty. It is possible that the law cited by Aeschines was not in force in 384 B.C. when the Theomnestus case was tried. And it was always possible in a criminal case to proceed by way of impeachment before the assembly. The assembly never surrendered to the heliastic courts its fundamental constitutional right to try any public offender. And there were certain features of an impeachment that made it attractive to a prosecutor.

It is manifest that the Athenians took precautions to safeguard freedom of speech by disqualifying, or otherwise punishing, citizens who abused it. The provisions fall into two classes. First are those intended to deprive unworthy men of the right to advise and influence their fellow-citizens in public. This purpose was achieved partly by subjecting to scrutiny at the will of any citizen those who habitually spoke in the public assemblies if they were suspected of specified offenses. The other provisions were intended to punish overt acts, such as deceiving the people, giving bad advice, and promoting inexpedient or unconstitutional legislation. The underlying purpose of these wise provisions was to make orators personally responsible for their public utterances just as magistrates were held responsible for their public acts.

But no laws or penalties could have fully enforced responsibility for public utterances. Nor was it desirable. Leadership and initiative on the part of popular leaders must be encouraged. Popular government would have languished and failed if every citizen stood in danger of the law every time he ventured to speak in public. Freedom of speech in Athens corresponds closely to freedom of the press in the modern world. It could neither be suppressed nor unduly restricted. That the Athenians were at least successful in impressing upon their orators a lively sense of their responsibility, would seem to be indicated by the words of an orator reported by Thucydides:[44]

In view of the very great interests at stake, and in so grave a matter, we who advise must regard it as our duty to look somewhat further ahead than you who give matters only a brief consideration, especially since we are responsible advisers, while you are irresponsible listeners. Indeed, if not only those who gave advice but also those who followed it had to suffer alike, you would show greater prudence in your decisions; but as it is, whenever you meet with a reverse you give way to your first impulse, and punish your adviser for his single error of judgment instead of yourselves, the multitude who shared in the error.

Diodotus here broadly hints that the multitude themselves are equally responsible with their adviser for mistakes in public policy, and Thucydides,[45] in speaking of the revulsion of feeling of the people against the politicians who were responsible for the Sicilian expedition, remarks that the people seemed to have forgotten that they themselves had voted for it. This view has recently been criticized. It has been maintained that "the theory of political responsibility, i.e., the responsibility of the statesman for the policy he advocates, was imperfectly understood by the ancient mind."[46] There is some truth in this criticism. But it is a serious mistake to go to the other extreme and absolve the people of any democracy, ancient or modern, from all political responsibility, and to put the blame wholly upon the politicians or the press.

CHAPTER V

CITIZENSHIP

CITIZENSHIP in an ancient Greek city was a precious asset; the loss of it was little short of a calamity. The value attached to the rights and privileges of citizenship is manifested by the practice of punishing crimes and misdemeanors by the restriction or withdrawal of citizenship from the convicted criminal. It would be tedious to make a list of the kinds of offense punished in this way. But it may be interesting to quote the *locus classicus* on disfranchisement complete or partial, found in Andocides, *On the Mysteries*.[1]

After the defeat of Aegospotamoi (405 B.C.), the Athenians decided to restore full rights to all whose civil and political rights had been abridged or withdrawn. The beneficiaries, says Andocides, included those who were in debt to the treasury because they had been convicted of malversation of public funds while in office, or failure to satisfy a judgment, or to pay fines and penalties, or to pay the money for franchises they had leased, or to make good their obligations as sureties. If they failed to pay by a specified date (on the ninth prytany) the amount was doubled and their property sold to satisfy their obligations to the treasury. If the property was insufficient, they and their descendants became *atimoi*.

Another type of disability consisted of loss of political rights without confiscation of property. In the class thus punished were those who had been convicted of embezzlement or bribery, of avoiding military service, or of cowardice, or of keeping their ships out of action, or of throwing away their shields, or of false testimony, or false summoning on the third offense, or of ill-using their parents. Still another class suffered a partial *atimia*. Specific disabilities were inflicted upon them. Among these were prohibitions to speak in the assembly, to be members of the council, and to bring criminal actions in the courts.

In the ancient world aliens were not readily admitted to citizenship. In the modern world a resident alien is generally admitted to citizenship on easy conditions, but if he does not choose to avail himself of the opportunity, his duties and his privileges are not markedly different from those of the citizen, and his children born within the boundaries of the state are *ipso facto* citizens, if they choose to be. In ancient Athens the situation was quite different. The position of the alien, whether transient or resident, was in no wise comparable to that of the citizen, and his children, though born in Attica, were like himself aliens nevertheless. In the early history of Athens there were occasions on which aliens had been freely admitted to citizenship. But in the fifth century, when the spoils of empire enhanced the value of citizenship, a law was passed restricting citizenship to those born of citizen parents.[2] The effect of the law was automatically to disfranchise all who could not prove that their parents were citizens. Aliens could be naturalized only by a vote of the assembly. As a rule only those who had rendered notable service to the state might expect such an honor.[3]

Athenian parents were responsible for the education of their children. A statement of Socrates[4] would seem to indicate that the law required a citizen to educate his sons, but there is no trace of such legislation. It is true that a boy who was not taught a trade by his father was excused from the obligation of supporting his parents in their old age.[5] But, in any event, it is certain that there was no system of state schools. Boys were sent to private schools escorted by a slave to guard them against harmful associations. The "three R's" of Athenian elementary education might be represented by three gammas, the initial letter of *grammata*, the letters of the alphabet which were used as figures as well as letters. Consequently a knowledge of *grammata* included reading, writing, and arithmetic.

Secondary education included music, poetry, and gymnastics. The learning of selections of poetry had a moral and a social purpose. They consisted for the most part in "admonitions and many praises and encomia of ancient famous men." Beyond the secondary school the further education of a boy depended largely upon the parent's means and the boy's inclination. Sophists of all kinds were ready for a consideration to give them a higher education. Though the curriculum embraced philosophy, mathematics, physics, astronomy, rhetoric, and dialectic, the main emphasis was laid upon rhetoric. This was natural in a community where ability to speak in public was so desirable.

The question of military training for Athenian youths presents some difficulties. Aristotle, in the *Constitution of Athens*,[6] describes an elaborate system of training for young men between the ages of eighteen and twenty. They were known as *ephebi*, the transliterated Greek word ἔφηβοι, or cadets. It used to be supposed that the military education of the cadets went back to the fifth century, but shortly after the recovery of Aristotle's work on the Athenian constitution, Wilamowitz argued so convincingly for the fourth-century organization of the cadets after the battle of Chaeronea in 338 B.C. that his date 335-4 has been very generally accepted.[7] A few remain unconvinced.

It doubtless is true that the system described by Aristotle is a typical fourth-century scheme. But it by no means follows that it was an entirely new institution. It is difficult to imagine that military training was left wholly to private enterprise until after the decisive Macedonian victory at Chaeronea. Individuals could be taught to handle weapons, but drill and field evolutions could be taught only to men

in military formations. Yet supporters of the view of Wilamowitz, in their zeal to disprove the earlier existence of
ephebic training, have cited at least two passages which
seem to indicate that Athenian youths received no organized military training whatever. Isocrates[8] is cited as saying, "We are unwilling to take the field, and while we
undertake war, I may say, against the whole world, we are
at no pains to prepare ourselves for it." And the Xenophontic Socrates is quoted as saying, "Military training is
not publicly recognized by the state."[9] These are exag-
gerated statements. Pericles pays little attention to military matters in the funeral speech, but does say, "We are
superior to our opponents in our system of training for
warfare."[10] His boast that the Athenian military forces
were not inferior to the Peloponnesians in the field has
usually been taken *cum grano salis*. But imperial Athens
could not have built up her empire and held it for three-
quarters of a century, with scarcely a breathing spell from
war, without well trained recruits.

One incident in Athenian warfare of this period is interesting in this connection. In 458 B.C. the Corinthians,
hoping to force the Athenians to withdraw their army from
the island of Aegina, which they were attempting to conquer, made a descent into the territory of Megara, then
held by the Athenians. But the Athenians met the challenge by sending out Myronides "with such forces as were
left in the city, consisting of the youngest and oldest men."[11]
These mixed troops succeeded in holding their own against
the regular Corinthian forces. Were these young men wholly
without cadet training? It does not seem probable.

There is another matter that has not been given due
weight in this discussion. The cadets, whose training Aristotle discusses so fully, took an oath of citizenship at the
end of their first year of training, when they received their
arms in the theater. The oath is as follows:

I will never bring reproach on my hallowed arms, nor will I desert the comrade at whose side I stand, but I will defend our altars and our hearths, single-handed or supported by many. My native land I will not leave a diminished heritage, but greater and better than when I received it. I will obey whoever is in authority and submit to the established laws and all others which the people shall harmoniously enact. If anyone tries to overthrow the constitution or disobeys it, I will not permit him, but will come to its defense single-handed or with the support of all. I will honor the religion of my fathers. Let the gods be my witnesses, Agraulus, Enyalius, Ares, Zeus, Thallo, Auxo, Hegemone.[12]

It is admitted by everybody that the oath goes back to the fifth century or earlier, and that it was taken upon enrollment in the catalogue of hoplites.[13] It is in part a military oath and could have been administered only to men who had received military training or expected to receive it. Consequently it would be wiser to assume that young men between the ages of eighteen and twenty always received some sort of cadet training in democratic Athens. With the advent of the mercenary soldier in the fourth century the system may very well have deteriorated seriously. The perilous condition of the city after Chaeronea naturally drove the citizens to make the best use of their military material by putting the cadet training on a sound basis. It is this revised system that Aristotle describes.

The oath bound the citizen to defend the state against foreign foes, to obey the authorities and the laws, to uphold the constitution, and to honor the ancestral religion. These were no light obligations in ancient Greece, where every neighboring city was a potential enemy, and where every form of government had at one time or another met serious and often successful attempts to change it by force or fraud. Frequently foreign and domestic foes united to overthrow the government.

Solon tried to strengthen the government against sedition, or *stasis*, as the Greeks called it, by requiring every citizen to take one side or another in case of serious party strife.[14] The penalty was loss of citizenship. The advantage expected from such a measure was that the full force of public opinion could be mobilized in an internal crisis. The indifferent were forced to declare themselves. It is doubtful if such a law could ever be made effective. Solon himself obeyed it by appearing in arms in front of his house, to back up with his feeble force his protest against the designs of Pisistratus, which he had voiced in the popular assembly.[15]

The aristocratic government that succeeded the monarchy in Athens depended upon the loyalty of the noble families grouped in clans whose members derived from a common ancestor, and brotherhoods or phratries composed of families whose estates were contiguous. It was these aristocrats who taught the lesson of service to the state as an object of ambition. It was a lesson easily learned in an organization in which there was social equality, but when Solon joined together in the service of the state the rich and the poor, the noble and the humble, with the distinctions of birth and wealth sharply marked, it was no easy task to establish a common loyalty to the state and to teach the lesson of public service. Solon was well aware of the difficulty of founding a composite state and uniting the aristocratic and popular factions in its service. "That city is best," he is reported to have said, "in which those who are not wronged are as zealous in prosecuting and punishing wrongdoers as those who are wronged."[16]

As democracy grew it is to the credit of many an aristocrat that he faithfully and loyally served the democracy in positions of danger and trust. And it is to the credit of democracy that it trusted its aristocrats with authority. By the middle of the fifth century the Athenians had become a nation with a strong *sensus communis*. There was privilege for none and opportunity for all.

In those offices [says Pseudo-Xenophon][17] which bring security to the whole commons if they are in the hands of good citizens, but if not, ruin, the commons desires to have no share. They do not think they ought to have a share through the lot in the supreme command or in the cavalry command, for the commons realizes that it reaps a greater benefit by not having these offices in its own hands, but by allowing men of standing to hold them.

Pericles, in the Funeral Oration, pointed out that

a man is preferred to public honors not because he belongs to a particular class, but because of personal merits; nor, again, on the ground of poverty is a man barred from public career by obscurity of rank if he has it in him to do the state a service.[18]

Athenian democracy, by its sound political sense and fair dealing, achieved a degree of harmony and coöperation in the state that was unusual in Greek city-states. In its hour of victory over the Thirty Tyrants and their aristocratic supporters it decided to forgive and forget, and to forego that vengeance which the victors in civil strife elsewhere always exacted.[19] The amnesty of 403 B.C. showed that the Athenians were ever ready to put the safety of the state above all other considerations.

It is admitted by Pseudo-Xenophon[20] that few were unjustly disfranchised in Athens. This is significant when it is remembered that exiles from Greek cities were constantly intriguing and scheming to overthrow the government by foreign aid. One of the lessons taught by this essay is that there was no hope of overthrowing democracy in this characteristic Greek fashion. In 411 B.C. democracy was overthrown by appealing to moderate opinion in the beginning. At the end of the war it was overthrown by the victors as a guaranty of peace. There was no *coup d'état* by political exiles.

The philosophy of the relationship of the citizen to the state has been well stated by Pericles.[21]

A state confers a greater benefit upon its private citizens when as a whole commonwealth it is successful, than when it prospers as regards the individual but fails as a community. For even though a man flourishes as regards his private fortune, yet if his country goes to ruin he perishes with her all the same; but if he is in evil fortune and his country in good fortune, he is far more likely to come through safely.

Solon's division of the population into four classes on a property basis was for the gradation of offices. The higher magistracies were limited to the upper classes, but by Aristotle's time even the lowest class was admitted tacitly to the highest office. The Solonian property standard was agricultural. Grain was valuable in a state which did not produce enough food to supply its own needs. And the produce of the olive and the vine could always be exported to supply the deficiency. Manufactures and commerce grew apace; but in the fourth century, through lack of daily sustenance men were compelled to take to foreign military service.[22] Nearly three decades of war made the trade of soldiering easy. But whatever the source of wealth and however it was distributed, there were always the rich and the poor. "Oligarchs" and "democrats" are but the political equivalents for the economic designations "rich" and "poor."

The struggle for control by these two groups of population was actuated by political motives; but back of these was the economic necessity of the poor that urged them to get control of the government. So long as they could exploit the resources of the empire, things went well; but when the empire was destroyed by the Peloponnesian war the rich had to be taxed to furnish state pay and doles for the impoverished masses. The position of the masses was rendered still worse by the competition of slave labor in manufactures.[23] It is often said too hastily that by reason of the institution of slavery Athenian democracy was really an aristocracy, with no manual labor to perform and plenty of leisure for the business of government. It is true that a large proportion of its members were men of independent means whose money was the product of capital invested in slaves; but slavery was a tool that cut both ways. While it enriched the few, it impoverished the many. It is this condition which gave a socialistic turn to Athenian democracy. In temperament the Greek was too much of an individualist to make a good socialist. In the *Parliament of Women* (392 B.C.), Aristophanes makes merry with the idea of community of property, but a few years later in the *Plutus*, where property is redistributed on the basis of worth, he is in a more serious mood. Poverty was becoming too widespread to be a jest for the rank and file of the citizens.

The only public duties required of a citizen were military service and the payment of taxes according to financial ability. All citizens had to serve in one or another branch of the army. The cavalry was recruited from the wealthier class, who had sufficient means to keep horses. These knights, numbering about one thousand, did not constitute a very important military organization in the wars of a maritime power. All other men fit for service were enrolled in the classes as they came of age. They served from the age of eighteen to sixty. The younger and the older men were normally not required to serve beyond the borders of Attica. The last year of military service was commuted for service as public arbitrators, after the introduction of public arbitration at the end of the fifth century.

There were penalties for failure to respond to the familiar summons to appear for military duty with three days' rations, for cowardice and desertion, and for throwing away arms. There were no decorations or rewards for bravery. The Greek soldier ran the risk not only of wounds and death, but of slavery if captured. The fate of the Athenians who surrendered in Sicily is still remembered. Visitors to Syracuse can still see the quarries where they worked and died. But this was exceptional. A captured soldier could usually buy his freedom, if he had the means or could borrow the money. The state would exchange prisoners of war, although public funds were not used to ransom them. But citizens of means often ransomed prisoners of war in a spirit of patriotism.

No public monuments were reared over those who died in battle. Their names were inscribed by tribes on stone slabs. A number of these casualty lists still survive.[24] Their bones were interred at an annual public funeral and a eulogy was delivered by a chosen orator, and their children were reared at the expense of the state.

The system of taxation had some unusual features that should be understood if one is to appreciate the obligations of citizenship. The Athenians had no protective tariff, but they did pay indirect taxes of various kinds. Property taxes under democracy were unknown until the revolt of Mytilene in 429 B.C. put a severe strain on the financial reserves of the city. The heaviest burden of taxation fell upon the richer citizens, who were required to expend large sums in the performance of public services called liturgies. The assignment and rotation of liturgies was not always satisfactory to those concerned. But there was a remedy. The dissatisfied individual could select one whom he deemed wealthier than himself and challenge him to accept the liturgy or exchange property with the challenger until the liturgy was performed. If the challenges were rejected the question was settled by the courts.

The better known of these services are the *choregia*, which involved the training of a dramatic chorus for the religious festivals, and the *trierarchia*, which involved the keeping of a warship in commission for a campaign. Originally some of these services were no doubt voluntary, but under democracy they were organized and arranged in such a fashion that no man of means could escape them; they were as inevitable as the other forms of taxation. But they still retained some elements of benevolence that made them seem less burdensome and irksome. The normal taxes were expended by state officials, but the liturgy was financed by the individual citizen. He expended the money himself. For the purpose in hand he was the representative of the state. He was thereby marked off from the other citizens. Under such circumstances it is not surprising that ambitious or public-spirited citizens performed their services in a splendid and even lavish manner. Cimon is said to have performed his liturgies "magnificently." His public liberality is further shown in his keeping open house for any of his fellow-demesmen who cared to come. This generous spirit brought him prestige and political influence.

Litigants were in the habit of referring to the liturgies they performed, in the expectation of winning the favor of the dicasts.[25] Indeed, one litigant even says that he was generous in his expenditures in order that he might profit by them if he was ever involved in litigation. These frank statements show quite clearly that men of means acquired merit in public opinion by their generosity. Sometimes a citizen went beyond legal requirements by performing two liturgies at the same time, by not waiting his turn, or by assuming the entire expense when the law permitted another to share it with him. On the other hand, a stingy and penurious performance of a liturgy, especially the *choregia*, brought public discredit upon a man.

The liturgies, as they were administered and regarded in Athens, afforded the wealthier citizens a well recognized means of making gifts and contributing benevolences to the state. For the citizens of lesser means there were voluntary gifts known as *epidoseis*, that is, gifts over and above the property tax.[26] One of the earliest references to an *epidosis* is that of Alcibiades on his first appearance in the assembly, when donations to the state were being collected. The practice was doubtless borrowed from the clubs, of which there were many in Athens. These were financed by gifts and contributions of the members. Sometimes they possessed endowments given by wealthy members. Men of means were often chosen as officers in the expectation that they would contribute generously to the finances of the organization. There were always more or less regular collections, and appeals for funds, which were in the nature of fees and assessments.

The origin of the *epidosis* shows very clearly the Athenian attitude toward the state. It was regarded as an organization which consulted the interests of its membership, just like a big club. It is this spirit which distinguishes the Athenian ideal of citizenship from modern conceptions of the state.

There were many public services expected of an Athenian citizen in addition to paying taxes and defending his fatherland, but they were not obligatory. Aristotle[27] estimates that there were seven hundred officials in Attica and a like number overseas during the period of the empire. There were also six thousand dicasts. All these officials were drawn by lot, as we have seen. In all probability the offices were filled from volunteers who presented themselves. But when these failed, the state had a right to draft candidates. This is a fair inference from the fact that there was a rotation of offices. No man could hold the same office twice except that of councilor. The exception was due to the fact that the annual drawing of five hundred councilors would exhaust the list of citizens in the lifetime of a man. The ordinary citizen was glad to hold office for the pay attached to it if for no other reason. Similarly, when dicasts were paid, there was no lack of full panels. Attendance at the meetings of the assembly presented difficulties to the authorities until pay for this service also was provided. Many devices, we are told, were used to induce the citizens to attend. One was to sweep the market place with a freshly painted rope and drive the loiterers into the neighboring Pnyx, where the meetings were held.[28]

In spite of the large number of public officials the citizen was expected to perform for himself services that in a modern community are performed at the public expense. If they were neglected the individual was the chief if not the only sufferer. For example, the streets were neither lighted nor patroled at night. The individual was responsible for his own protection against thieves, pickpockets, kidnapers, and other kinds of criminals that were abroad after nightfall. Men of means had torch-bearers and other attendant slaves. The humble citizen had to protect himself as best he could or remain indoors.

In private litigation a citizen was expected to do many things for himself that are done nowadays by lawyers and court bailiffs and sheriffs. After entering his case with the proper magistrate, accompanied by two witnesses known as summoners, he notified the defendant to appear and file an answer to the charges or claims. In theory he secured his own witnesses and worked up his case and presented it in court, but in practice he could avail himself of the services of a professional speech-writer to compose a speech for him to deliver in court. If he won his case, the judgment was not turned over to an official, like the modern sheriff, for execution. The winner must himself execute the judgment, at his own expense. When an official proceeds to seize chattels to satisfy a judgment, he has behind him the majesty of the law. Resistance to his authority is a crime or a misdemeanor. But when the plaintiff himself has to go to the premises of the defendant and make a seizure the situation is entirely different. The bitterness engendered by litigation not infrequently resulted in violence. The only remedy for the plaintiff, if he was assaulted, was to enter a suit for assault and battery and embark on further litigation. The system of self-service was based upon the principle that the state should do nothing for its citizens which they could do for themselves. It had its disadvantages, but it tended to make men self-reliant, and it fitted them to serve the state and their fellow-citizens.

The administration of criminal justice depended entirely upon volunteers. The system originated with Solon. When Solon relieved the masses of some of their burdens and protected them by law from exploitation at the hands of the landed gentry, from whose ranks the higher magistrates were drawn, it was quite unlikely that the downtrodden lower classes either would or could avail themselves of the protection of the law by resorting to litigation under existing conditions. He met this difficulty by permitting anyone who wished to intervene and prosecute any wrongdoer, even if he himself was in no wise injured by the wrongdoing. Whether or not Solon's reliance upon volunteers was immediately justified we have no means of knowing. But in the fifth century the volunteer prosecutor was thoroughly established. The system worked. There was always a sufficiency of amateur prosecutors. The motives that actuated the volunteer accuser were many. Litigation, as we have seen, was the ready weapon of the practical politician against his opponents. Litigation offered a means of vengeance upon one's personal enemies that met with public approval. In certain types of cases the volunteer was encouraged to come forward by the prospect of sharing the moneys recovered by the state or the fines inflicted, if he was able to prove his charges. There was an action known as "denunciation"[29] employed in cases of infractions of customs or mining laws. The prosecutor obtained one-half of the property confiscated or the fine levied. A form of

67570

action known as "inventory"[30] was employed to recover confiscated property that was concealed by the collusion of relatives. The prosecutor received three-fourths of the amount recovered.

Provisions for the apprehension of criminals seem to us very inadequate. Criminals known as "malefactors," including thieves, cut-purses, house-robbers, clothes-snatchers and kidnapers, might be summarily arrested *in flagrante delicto* and haled before the Eleven by anyone. Instead of arresting the criminal, the citizen might point him out to a magistrate or lodge a written complaint and leave further action to the authorities. If any such case came to trial, the citizen responsible for the apprehension of the criminal acted both as prosecuting attorney and complaining witness. He was apparently not liable to reprisals in the nature of an action for false arrest if the accused was wrongfully put on trial. But if he failed to receive one-fifth part of the votes of the dicasts he was fined one thousand drachmas. This fine was inflicted in practically all cases so as to discourage unfounded charges. An exception was made in impeachments. They were tried by the assembly itself or referred by a decree to the heliastic court. The reason for the exception was that the assembly, by accepting the case, relieved the prosecutor of responsibility.

Homicide was not treated as a crime so far as the procedure was concerned. The trial was classed as a private suit, and only relatives of the deceased up to second cousins could prosecute. If these failed to take action the murderer, if discovered, could be summarily arrested by anyone, as a polluted person who, contrary to the proclamation of the king archon, had frequented public places. By this means the exclusive right of relatives to prosecute was technically preserved.

For distinguished services to the state there were honors and rewards. But comparatively few achieved them. The right to sit in a front seat at the theatrical productions and public games was sometimes bestowed upon successful generals. Aristophanes[31] says that formerly the *proedria*, as this honor was called, was always the reward of merit; but nowadays politicians like Cleon used their influence to get the privilege for their friends.

Another honor closely associated with the *proedria* was the privilege of dining daily in the Prytaneum where the *prytaneis* had their meals. Socrates, after being adjudged guilty, was required to present to the jury, according to Athenian criminal procedure, an alternative punishment to the death penalty demanded by the prosecutors. He boldly proposed that, as a public benefactor, he should not be punished, but rewarded by free meals at the Prytaneum. Surely he had done a greater service to the city than had successful athletes who were invited to dine with the *prytaneis* upon their return from Olympia.[32]

Normally there was no reward for the magistrates beyond their pay. But the councilors were assigned to a reserved section in the theater. On the conclusion of their term of office each councilor received a crown if the audit was passed. Other boards could be so honored by a vote of the people. Individuals also might be voted a crown in appreciation of distinguished services to the city. Such was the crown voted to Demosthenes. In defense of the legality of the vote the most famous speech in history was delivered, the oration *On the Crown*.

For the rank and file of Athenian citizens the material rewards and emoluments were not large. Besides pay for service in the army or the navy, all officials, including dicasts, received stipends. In the fourth century indemnities were paid for attendance at the meetings of the assembly. The sums of money thus disbursed throughout the citizen body were very welcome and among the poorer citizens helped materially to make both ends meet. There is mention in the sources of a sum of two obols paid to citizens daily. The purpose of the payment is not known. It was probably a dole paid out to needy and impoverished citizens who were not on the public pay roll.[33]

The state cared for indigent cripples. There was a law which enacted that persons possessing less than three minas (about fifty dollars) who were so crippled as to be unable to do any work· should, after examination by the council, receive two obols a day for their support. If a cripple was not wholly incapacitated, the allowance was reduced to one obol. Cripples in receipt of state aid could be called upon to appear before the council and prove their infirmities.[34] One of the most amusing of the clients of Lysias was a cripple with a sharp tongue, put upon his defense before the council by a citizen who doubted his need of public help.

In Athens, as in modern democracies, public opinion was a potent factor. A citizen who shirked his public duties in Athens incurred the blame of his fellow-citizens. "We alone," says Pericles, "regard a man who takes no interest in public affairs not as a harmless but as a useless person." The word which is here rendered "harmless" has implications and connotations which no single English word can reproduce. In certain connections it may be rendered "inoffensive" or "peaceable." In others it may be rendered as "shirker" or "slacker." As used by Pericles[35] it carried a reproach which few men would willingly incur.

Attendance on meetings of the assembly, participation in the discussions, prosecuting criminals, appearing as a candidate for allotment to office, performing public services generously and gladly, are some of the marks of the "useful" as distinguished from the "useless" citizen.

But there was always a danger that the useful citizen, in his zeal for public service, would become over-zealous and therefore obnoxious to his fellow-citizens. Such a person

was known as *polypragmon* ("meddlesome," "officious").
Socrates, in his zeal to test the accuracy of the oracle that
proclaimed him to be the wisest man, went about the city
examining all and sundry who had a reputation for wisdom.
This procedure won him many enemies and the general reputation of being *polypragmon*. "Why," said the Athenians,
"if he was so anxious to spend his days giving counsel to
individuals, did he not appear in the assembly and let the
state have the benefit of his wisdom?"[36]

The most notorious example of over-zealousness in the
public service was the volunteer public prosecutor, who
made it a profession to prosecute and even to blackmail
his fellow-citizens, often on groundless charges. Such men
were known as "sycophants." It was difficult to check sycophants without discouraging the honest public prosecutor
upon whose efforts the administration of justice depended.
In this respect, freedom of prosecution in Athens resembles
freedom of the press in modern communities. The public
advantage of free criticism is so great that we are willing
to allow the press almost untrammeled liberty. The checks
upon sycophancy were inadequate. The only effective cure
for the abuse would have been the substitution of public,
for volunteer, prosecutors. But the delegation of authority
was contrary to the spirit of Greek democracy. Even Plato
in the *Laws*[37] made no provision for a public prosecutor.

In a monarchy the loyalty of the citizen is his devotion
to the person of his sovereign. In an aristocracy or any type
of oligarchy the state depends upon the class loyalty of its
limited citizenry. But in a democracy there is neither an
individual nor a ruling class to inspire loyalty. Just what
inspired the loyalty of an Athenian? Let us see what Pericles had to say in his memorable Funeral Oration, which,
unlike the typical speech delivered on such occasions, presented an ideal picture of democratic Athens to inspire
anew the loyalty of its citizens, faced as they were with the

dangers of war. "Day by day," he says, "fix your eyes upon the greatness of Athens, until you become filled with the love of her."[38] The immediately succeeding words show that he has in mind imperial Athens, mistress of one hundred and fifty cities. But the imperial power of the city was not the sole reason for the loyalty and devotion of its sons. There was respect for law and duly constituted authority. "We render obedience to those in authority and to the laws." Most especially did they regard those laws that were enacted for the succor of the oppressed. As a result all men were "on an equality for the settlement of their private disputes."

Athens did not neglect the things of the spirit, as we moderns know so well. But Pericles did not labor the point. There was no need of this before an audience who year after year heard those great dramas which are still regarded as literary masterpieces, and daily saw those monuments of architecture that are the admiration of the modern world. "We have provided for the spirit many relaxations from toil; we have games and sacrifices regularly throughout the year, and homes fitted out with good taste and elegance."

In both a material and a spiritual sense Athens achieved as did no other Greek city that self-sufficiency so highly esteemed in ancient Hellas.[39] "Our city is equally admirable in peace and in war. . . . It is so great that all the products of the earth flow in upon us. . . . Each individual amongst us could in his own person, with the utmost grace and versatility, prove himself self-sufficient in the most varied forms of activity."

Citizens of Athens knew each other much better than do the inhabitants of a modern city of similar size. Practically every citizen was born and reared in Attica. His first associations were with the little group he met in school and afterwards in the gymnasium. Other associations he formed in the phratry as he grew to manhood. He always was regarded as a resident of the deme in which he was born, and he was closely associated with his fellow-demesmen in the local assemblies that administered the government. These home associations were always first outside the family. Then there were the military organization by tribes and the tribal assemblies that enlarged his contacts beyond the phratry and the deme. Residents of the city and its environs who had the requisite leisure spent much time in the shops about the *agora*, where they discussed all sorts of things and heard the news, both domestic and foreign. Athens had no newspapers or magazines to inform the public and mold public opinion. It is a pity that no contemporary writer has left us a record of the discussions in these clearing houses of public opinion. Plato has preserved the spirit of such meetings of members of the upper classes in his dialogues. And both Plato and Xenophon have described the more formal after-dinner meetings known as *symposia*. Along with songs, jests, and stories, there was always a vein of more or less serious discussion.

In a speech attributed to Demosthenes[40] there is preserved an interesting and instructive account of the trials and tribulations of a citizen who was called upon to serve the state in the Athenian way. In the fifth century the burden of keeping a warship in commission had been undertaken independently by individuals under the supervision of the generals. But in 357-6 B.C. a new plan was introduced because there were not enough wealthy individuals to keep the ships in commission. The twelve hundred richest men in the state were divided into twenty groups of sixty each, known as trierarchic symmories. The burden was distributed among these symmories. On one occasion there was a serious lack of naval equipment. None could be bought in the Piraeus. To meet the emergency vigorous measures were taken to recover from the trierarchs the ships' tackle which had not been turned in to the naval authorities. To this end a decree was passed according to which the names of the delinquents were assigned proportionately by lot to the twenty members of the symmories designated to help the generals to administer the system. They were instructed to secure the equipment. The client of Demosthenes was both a trierarch and an overseer. He was instructed to secure equipment from two men who had acted as joint trierarchs and had not turned in the equipment belonging to the state. Their names were Demochares and Theophemus. Both refused to accede to his request. The speaker commenced action for recovery. He had no option in the matter. He won a verdict and Demochares produced his share of the tackle, but Theophemus refused, hoping that the speaker, who had to take out a warship, would have to provide his own tackle. "Finding that I could not get the ship's furniture I applied to the clearing officers, the council, and the assembly, stating that Theophemus did not return the ship's furniture for which the court had pronounced him to be accountable." The speaker's case was not unique. Other trierarchs also applied to the council for help to get the equipment due them. The council passed a decree requiring them to collect the naval stores or their equivalent in whatsoever way they could.

Armed with this decree and accompanied by a servant of the council, the speaker proceeded to the house of Theophemus. On his refusing to satisfy the judgment, the speaker started to distrain some of his chattels. Theophemus resisted and a fight ensued. The speaker presented himself to the council again, exhibiting the evidence he bore of the assault. The council bade him impeach Theophemus in the assembly. The case was first heard in the council, according to practice. The charges were, delaying the departure of the fleet and assaulting a citizen while in the performance of his duty to the state. The speaker was

Remote

JC 73 . B6

1967

Aspects of
Athenian
Democracy

was found guilty and fined
ment. The damages for the
y private arbitration. The
erarch. On his return, failing
is agreement to arbitrate, he
ery. The answer of Theophe-
ssault and battery. Each liti-
r began the assault and was
is secured an adjournment of
eaker allowed the case against
t it by false testimony, as he
Being under the necessity of
asked Theophemus for time to
inst him. Theophemus refused
help of a relative, made a seizure
ttels. They were disappointed in
y secured, for the speaker asserts
d furniture had been pawned and
liberality in public service.

g was aggravated by the fact that
aded the quarters of the women, a
most scandalous   ut this was not all. They caused, by
their violence, the death of an old servant who sought to
protect her master's property. The servant was a freed-
woman, a former slave of the speaker. As she was neither a
slave nor a relative, he could not prosecute the murderer.
This was a great sorrow to him, as the woman had been his
nurse and the family was much attached to her. The next
day the speaker paid the amount of the judgment, but his
opponent refused to return the goods distrained unless he
would drop proceedings in a perjury suit against two witnesses in the suit for assault and battery which he had lost.

It is true that the story here summarized is an *ex parte*
statement, but it should be remembered that even if the
speaker was technically guilty of assault in distraining the

property of Theophemus, he was acting for the state to recover state property. Of this there can be no doubt. Furthermore, he was not the only citizen required at this time to replevy state property. Other trierarchs also, in addition to performing an expensive liturgy, were put to trouble and additional expense in getting the fittings of the ships they were to keep in commission on a war footing. The duties of citizenship, often onerous, might become distressing and even disastrous to a zealous citizen.

Pericles has painted a picture of a splendid democracy as he saw it. It is admittedly an ideal. Like the ideas of Plato, it was a pattern of democracy "laid up in heaven" for men to contemplate and strive to imitate. One needs no profound knowledge of the history of Pericles' times and the fourth century to realize that in many ways his fellow-citizens fell far short of his ideal. But at least we have evidence to show that one of his statements regarding the citizens of Athens cannot be gainsaid: "We love beauty and seek wisdom." It is probable that the Athenian voters never exceeded twenty-five thousand,[41] or thirty thousand at most. It is conceivable that from the upper strata of even so small a group there may have come a lawgiver and economist like Solon, a statesman like Pericles, a patriot-orator like Demosthenes, a sculptor like Pheidias, a philosopher like Plato, and poets like Aeschylus, Sophocles, and Aristophanes, to name only a few. These men created beauty and found wisdom. But it must not be forgotten that they had to have an audience, a constituency, a public who appreciated them. Otherwise they would have been mere voices crying in the wilderness. Their works would not have lived after them.

It was this city, where men "loved beauty and sought wisdom" which Pericles said was the "school of Hellas." In the fourth century Isocrates reiterated the claim, and to this day men have continued to go to Athens to school.

CHAPTER VI

LITERATURE

THE GENERATION which saw both the American and the French revolutions indulged in much speculation as to how democracy would affect letters and arts. Two distinct views were held. Liberal opinion expected that the new democracy would stimulate individual genius and call forth public appreciation of intellectual worth wherever it was discovered. Conservative opinion, on the contrary, believed that "political equality tends to depress originality and individuality, disparaging genius." "The tendency of democracy is to reduce all to the level of the average." Such speculations were interesting but valueless, because, as Lord Bryce[1] has pointed out, political conditions cannot be isolated from other influences at work. A review of history seems to indicate that political conditions have little to do with literature. It is a common view that in Greece and Rome literature flourished only so long as there was political and national liberty. In a great measure this is true, though the appearance of writers like Seneca, Pliny, Tacitus, Juvenal, and Martial in Rome under the Empire would seem to belie the view. In Hellas it is true that both oligarchy and democracy produced great philosophers and lyric poets, but the Golden Age of Athenian literature, from Aeschylus to Demosthenes, coincides very closely with the period of the democratic régime. The battle of Salamis (480 B.C.) at once saved Athenian democracy and served as an inspiration to the poet Aeschylus. His *Persians*, the earliest of the extant Athenian tragedies, celebrated the memorable defeat of the Persian hosts. And the unsuccessful struggle against Macedonia spelled the doom of democracy and inspired Demosthenes, the last of the great Athenian orators. These coincidences are not without significance. One of the most striking and instructive features of Greek literature is the fact that it immediately and unmistakably reflected, as does no other literature, the political, social, and economic conditions under which it was produced. No literary type exemplifies this feature better than Attic oratory, a distinctive product of Athenian democracy.

Wherever men are politically organized on terms of equality there is constant need of speech and discussion. Even under the aristocratic monarchy depicted by Homer, oratory was essential. The nobles, in council with the king, debated questions of policy. In the assembly any free man might discuss matters of public interest. Homeric oratory belongs to the deliberative type; it is the oratory of debate. The popularity of the Homeric poems familiarized the Greeks with deliberative oratory in poetic form. It is, therefore, not surprising that Solon,[2] who was a poet as well as a statesman, chose to recite a poem in the *agora* instead of delivering an oration, when he wished to stir the populace to recover the island of Salamis from the Megarians.

In the days of Solon and for long afterwards oratory was a faculty or natural gift, which could be improved by practice; it was not an art that could be taught. The art of rhetoric was developed in Sicily about the middle of the fifth century B.C., in the throes of political and social reorganization that followed the overthrow of the tyrants. Corax, a successful politician of Syracuse, came to realize that his speeches consisted of three parts, viz., the proem, in which he sought to gain the good will of his audience and an attentive hearing; the narrative and argumentative portion, which he called λόγος; and finally the epilogue (ἐπίλογος), which consisted of a summary of the arguments advanced and an appeal. On this simple basis the art of oratory was founded. Eloquence ceased to be a gift of the favored few; it became an art that could be taught.

One would naturally suppose that the deliberative oratory of the council and the assembly would be standardized and developed before the forensic oratory of the law courts. But such was not the fact. Extant forensic speeches go back to the fifth century, but the documentary history of deliberative or parliamentary oratory begins with Demosthenes' speech *On the Navy Boards* in 354 B.C. The explanation of this situation is not far to seek. Solon required each litigant to plead his own case in court. Few men could do this unaided. The result was that men who lacked skill in public speech resorted for aid to experts, who familiarized themselves with the law and the evidence in the cases which they accepted, and prepared suitable speeches for their clients to recite in court. These speech-writers, or "logographs" as they were called, published many of their compositions for advertising purposes. The public was interested in them as models more than as literature. No doubt the logograph stood ready to compose deliberative speeches for clients; but a prepared speech could rarely be used in a debate. The politicians of the fourth and fifth centuries seem to have composed their own speeches, but apparently they did not publish them.

The orators and logographs found it necessary to develop a new medium of expression. The fifth-century Athenians were familiar with poetry, but of Attic prose they knew little or nothing. The earliest example of prose is the crudely phrased and badly organized essay on the Athenian democracy wrongly attributed to Xenophon.[3] Prose of this character was of little or no value to a public speaker in search of a suitable medium of expression. A speaker in the assembly would most naturally use the language of daily life, adorned by occasional poetic words, phrases, or concepts drawn from the great poets, much as the older generation in our own day seasoned their more formal speech with the language of the Bible. An example of this poetic element in the speeches of Pericles[4] is his comparison of the death of the young to a year without a spring.

Another element in deliberative oratory, found in reminiscences of Pericles' speeches, is the tendency to use proverbs, aphorisms, and apothegms, which formulate the wisdom gained by experience in simple homely fashion. An example is the comparison of the Samians to children who cry but take their food nevertheless, or the comparison of the internal troubles of Boeotia to an oak tree rent by wedges made of its own timber. Nothing is so effective in an argument as the use of one of these sententious sayings that have behind them the force of long tradition. There was available in the gnomic poets an excellent selection of suitable material.

This tendency often develops into a trick known as phrase-making, by which a clever speaker sums up an idea in a brief expression easily remembered. One feels that in the *Funeral Oration*, as reported by Thucydides, there are a few such *sententiae* that may well have been uttered by Pericles. The advice to women to act so as not to occasion comments among men either for good or for ill, and the statement that not avarice but love of honor is characteristic of old men,[5] may well be Periclean.

Closely akin to the practice of phrase-making is the power to concentrate the whole train of thought developed in a paragraph into a single word or phrase, such as Pericles' description of Ægina as "the eyesore of the Piraeus."[6] It is probable that the comic poet Eupolis[7] has this in mind when he says, "He alone of the orators left something behind like the sting of a bee."

Antiphon, the first Attic orator whose speeches are extant, achieved some success in devising a suitable medium of expression for forensic oratory, but his austere style was

unsuited to the courts, and he was practically debarred
from speaking because the people were suspicious of his
rhetorical cleverness.[8] It was Lysias who perfected a model
prose style for the courts, characterized as the "plain style"
by the ancient critics, as distinguished from the "austere
style" of Antiphon, or the "florid style" of Gorgias and
his successors. The popularity of Lysias is shown by the
fact that more than four hundred speeches were credited to
him in antiquity. When in a succeeding age men sought to
revive Attic simplicity, Lysias was regarded as the truest
representative. And Lysias was a product of the democratic system of the administration of justice.

A very important element in Attic prose style was contributed by Gorgias, one of the outstanding figures in the
history of Attic oratory. In 427 B.C. he arrived in Athens
as the spokesman of a political embassy from his native
city, Leontini, and his speech created a veritable sensation
with its "symmetry of clause, parallelism of structure, and
similarity of termination,"[9] characteristics quite foreign to
the oratory of Pericles, the master orator of the assembly
until his death in 429 B.C. The following selection from the
funeral oration of Gorgias[10] will serve better than any technical description to give an idea of the extravagant and
florid style of oratory that captivated the Athenians:

What was absent from these men that should be present, and
what was present that should be absent? Could I but say what I
wish and wish to say what I should, evading Nemesis from gods
and avoiding envy of men, for these possessed immortal valor
and human mortality! Much they preferred lenient fairness to
haughty justice and much also rightness of reason to rightness of
law, thinking this the most divine, the most universal law to
speak and to secrete, to commit and to omit in due season; employing two things most necessary, mind and might, the one in
advising, the other in realizing; cherishers of those unjustly unfortunate, and chastisers of those unjustly fortunate; unyielding

to the expedient, passionate for the right; with the wisdom of mind overcoming the unwisdom of might, insolent to the insolent, polite to the polite, fearless to the fearless, terrible in the midst of terrors. As testimonies of their tempers they set up trophies over their antagonists, images of Zeus, but mementos of themselves. Not without experience were they of natural war or lawful affections or armed strife or art-loving peace. Reverent toward the gods in justice, pious toward parents in nurture, just toward citizens in equality, faithful to their friends in loyalty were they. Therefore, though they are dead, our yearning for them in death has not died with them, but deathless in their dead images it lives on though they live not.

Only an audience educated in poetry and habituated to the poetic drama could ever have been thrilled by this florid, ornate prose, in which sound often predominates over sense. But they soon grew weary of it. It was left for Isocrates, a pupil of Gorgias, to select and use the valid elements in this style, and to fashion an artistic prose which through Cicero became the norm of modern prose style. Isocrates was not himself a public speaker, because of his timid nature and weak voice; but he was a teacher of orators. His contemporaries knew his style only through his political essays on matters of Hellenic interest, which he published in the form of speeches.

Oratory was extremely popular in Athens. In the same year that Gorgias as ambassador from his native Leontini created such a sensation, Thucydides[11] reports a speech of Cleon in the famous debate on the fate of Mytilene, in which he denounces the popular preoccupation with oratorical displays in the assembly:

Misled by clever speakers, the people make dangerous concessions to the subject states. The sophisticated members of the assembly ought rather to give good advice than to seek occasions for the display of eloquence and cleverness and become rivals in oratory for popular applause. In such rhetorical contests the city gives away the prizes to others while she takes the risk upon herself. And you are to blame for ordering these contests amiss. When speeches are to be heard you are too fond of using your eyes, but where actions are concerned you use your ears. You are slaves of each paradox and contemptuous of the familiar. Not a man of you but would be an orator if he could. In a word, you are at the mercy of your ears and sit like spectators attending a performance of sophists rather than counselors of state.

The extraordinary popular interest in oratory is further indicated by the publication of deliberative and epideictic orations in the fourth century for the use of the reading public. The publication of forensic speeches, as has been pointed out, was mainly for students of rhetoric.

Isocrates contrasts forensic oratory with the other two types[12] to the disadvantage of the former as follows: "Forensic speeches are a bore. They are tolerable only on the day of delivery." "Other orators are welcome in all assemblies. Their oratory from a literary point of view is superior, and audiences enjoy it as much as poetry." Isocrates is a prejudiced witness because of his hostility to the sophists, with whom he does not wish to be identified. But there is no doubt that there was a growing demand for the publication of deliberative and epideictic orations which culminated in the publication of deliberative orations delivered during the struggle with Macedonia.[13] Isocrates' own publications prove the popularity of oratory with the reading public. Although he never delivered a public address in his life, his political essays were all cast in the form of speeches purporting to have been delivered before the Athenian assembly, at the Panathenaic festival in Athens, or the Panhellenic gathering at Olympia. But the practice of Isocrates was not destined to develop a new literary type. An oration, composed for the eye rather than for the ear, labors under some very obvious disadvantages as a medium of publication.

Oratory exercised a very marked influence on the writing of history. It was inevitable that the historians should avail themselves of the medium of expression developed by the orators. Thucydides, the first Athenian historian, was a pupil of Antiphon, from whom he acquired the austere style. The influence of Gorgias in the narrative portions of his work is very faint. But the speeches, which constitute more than one-fifth of his history of the Peloponnesian war, quite distinctly reflect the influences of contemporary rhetoric. Thucydides was not the first writer to introduce set speeches into the body of his work. They are found in the epics of Homer and in the history of Herodotus. No Greek could record deeds without also recording words. But the dialogues, conversations, and speeches in Herodotus are a dramatic element in a work intended to be heard rather than read. Moreover, where the speeches are cast in the mold of a debate, as in the debate of the plotters who had put Smerdis to death, regarding the relative merits of monarchy, oligarchy, and democracy for Persia, they are not at all Persian. The arguments of Otanes for democracy, of Megabyzus for oligarchy, and of Darius for monarchy, are entirely Hellenic.[14] Thucydides,[15] on the other hand, reports real speeches, deliberative and diplomatic in the main. The "things said" ($\tau\grave{\alpha}$ $\lambda\epsilon\chi\theta\acute{\epsilon}\nu\tau\alpha$) are as distinctly a part of the story of the war as are the "things done" ($\tau\grave{\alpha}$ $\acute{\epsilon}\rho\gamma\alpha$). An Athenian like Thucydides, himself a member of the assembly which governed Athens, could not very well conceive of a story of the war otherwise. The speeches are both political, in that they are discussions of policy on critical occasions, and rhetorical, in that they are clothed in the rhetoric current in the last quarter of the fifth century, whether the language is that of Thucydides himself or of the speaker he reports.

Of subsequent Athenian historians little need be said beyond noting the marked influence which Isocrates had

on their style. Among his distinguished pupils were the
historians Theopompus and Ephorus. Even Xenophon in
the last five books of the *Hellenica* shows the influence of
Isocrates.[16] In this connection it may be noted that a substantial element in the success of the Ten Thousand was
due to the oratorical ability of Xenophon. "The accom-
plishments," says Grote,[17] "whereby Xenophon rendered
such services to his army [i.e., the Ten Thousand] were ac-
complishments belonging in an especial manner to Athenian
democracy and education." "Without the oratory of Xenophon there would have existed no engine for kindling or
sustaining the *sensus communis* of the Ten Thousand or of
keeping up the moral authority of the aggregate over the
individual members and factions."

The influence of democracy upon both tragedy and
comedy was marked, owing to the fact that the selection
and presentation of plays in democratic Athens was wholly
in the hands of the government. Thespis, a contemporary
of Solon, is said to have been the first to introduce tragedy
into Athens. It was purely a private enterprise, in which
the poet was both author and actor. The new form of
entertainment won popular favor, though Solon criticized
it severely, and asked Thespis "if he was not ashamed to
tell such lies in the presence of so many people."[18]

The earliest occurrence of state patronage of the drama
in Athens was a dramatic competition in which Thespis
took part and won the prize. The date was 534 B.C. At
this time Pisistratus was strongly entrenched in power in
Athens. The Pisistratidae, like others of the Greek tyrants,
were patrons of literature. Hipparchus invited to Athens
Anacreon, Simonides, and others. In connection with the
Ionic festival at Delos the Pisistratidae are said to have
regulated the recitations from Homer by having an edition
of the *Iliad* and the *Odyssey* published, which was thenceforth used by the rhapsodists at the celebration of the

festival.[19] Because of this reorganization of the Delian festival it has been plausibly conjectured that Pisistratus established or reorganized the City Dionysia, the festival in
honor of Dionysus Eleuthereus, and that he added com-
petitions in tragedy.[20]

On the expulsion of the Pisistratidae, democracy continued dramatic contests as part of the City Dionysia, and
became a patron of literature. The continuance of the practice was largely for religious reasons. Once a new part was
added to a religious celebration, it could not easily be abandoned. The audience in the Attic theaters was participating in an act of worship. Thus it happens that dramas were
presented only at the recurring festivals of Dionysus. Besides the Anthesteria, the Great or City Dionysia, and the
Lenaea celebrated in the city, there were the Rural Dionysia, which were celebrated in the larger demes.

The festival of the City Dionysia, the greatest of the
celebrations, began with a great religious procession in
which the ancient statue of Dionysus was carried through
the streets with great pomp and circumstance in com-
memoration of the introduction of the new cult. Everybody, even women and girls, participated. All citizens were
given an opportunity to attend the dramatic performances
that were held continuously throughout four or five days
of the festival. Poor citizens, who could not pay, were admitted free of charge. It is possible that women also were
allowed to attend, though there is not enough evidence
available to prove this. Some notion of the possible size of
the audience may be obtained from the fact that the
theater of Dionysus held approximately seventeen thousand people.

In addition to the audience of citizens there was a great
concourse of strangers from all parts of Greece. In the fifth
century the City Dionysia was made the occasion for a
great imperial display. Deputations came from the tribu-

tary states bringing the tribute. It was also a favorite season for the coming of embassies. These great audiences of citizens and strangers must have constituted a strong incentive to the poets to do their best.

In Athens the drama always retained its religious connection; it never became secularized as it did in other places in Greece. There were no private theatrical ventures or exhibitions. The drama was a state monopoly. The result was that, while the dramatists had an opportunity never equaled before or since of getting a nation-wide hearing for their works and of forming and educating public taste, they themselves had to be careful to conform to the prevailing standards. The system of competition not only furnished a stimulus to the poet to do his best, but it also gave an opportunity for expressing and registering public opinion on the verdict of the judges. The action and reaction of authors and audiences upon each other was immediate and unmistakable. All novelties in subject matter or treatment were at once brought to the test.

The state selected the competing plays and financed their production. A poet who wished to exhibit a drama had to submit his manuscript to the *archon eponymus*, if he wished to exhibit at the City Dionysia, to the *archon basileus*, if it was the Lenaea. If his application was favorably received, the proper archon "gave him a chorus," as the technical phrase ran. It was the business of the *choregus*, selected by the archon, to finance the drama and pay the chorus. The dramatic choruses were probably drawn from the ranks of professional singers. The poet was originally responsible for the training of the chorus. Hence he was called the "teacher" ($\delta\iota\delta\acute{\alpha}\sigma\kappa\alpha\lambda\sigma$).

Only three poets were allowed to compete in the City Dionysia.[21] The responsibility of deciding among the various applicants fell upon the archon. This was a serious responsibility. It was highly desirable that poets be selected who would satisfy the public. The expenditure of money upon staging a poor play would give occasion for criticism. That there was criticism is shown by the fact that the comic poet Cratinus[22] found fault with the archon for preferring Gnesippus, son of Cleomachus, to Sophocles. Aristophanes[23] refers to the failure of the comic poets Morsimus and Melanthius to obtain choruses as if it were a matter of common occurrence. But beyond criticism there was nothing to be done about it. The archon would never again be in office to profit by the criticism. It is true, the matter might be raised by the *euthyna*, but the complainant would have to prove some corrupt motive, for bad taste in literature was not a punishable offense in Athens.[24] Just how the Athenians could expect to secure by lot each year two competent or even tolerable literary critics is not clear. The importance of this preliminary selection of poets, each of whom would receive a prize, was so great that the lexicographer Suidas said that to gain a chorus was equivalent to winning a victory.

In contrast with the curious and casual manner in which the competing poets were selected, stands the careful selection of the judges who were to determine the merit of the plays selected and presented.[25] A preliminary list of judges was drawn up secretly by the council and the *choregi*. From this list ten were drawn by lot in the theater by the archon before the performances began. These ten observed the performance and gave their verdicts in writing. From these ten lists of the competing poets arranged in order of merit, five were selected by lot. On the basis of these five lists the final verdict was determined. All these precautions were taken to prevent attempts to influence the judges in favor of a particular candidate.

The audience in the Athenian theater, like the members of the assembly and the law courts, did not hesitate to mark their approval or disapproval of a performance.[26]

Their attitude could not have failed to influence the judges, so that in a sense the final verdict regarding the respective merits of the poets chosen by the archon was really the verdict of the audience, which was not a select group of playgoers but a cross-section of the populace of Athens. It is a great mark of the excellence of the literary taste of the Athenian democracy that in tragedy they selected for continuous approval three such men as Aeschylus, Sophocles, and Euripides.

In the fifth and fourth centuries the themes of tragedy were drawn from the rich store of Greek myths. But Phrynichus, who obtained his first tragic victory in 512 B.C., had made an attempt to dramatize contemporary history. His first play of this character dealt with the capture and destruction of Miletus in 494 in the Ionic revolt. The Athenians, in resentment at being reminded so vividly of their sorrow at the failure of the revolt, for which they had had much sympathy and some responsibility, fined Phrynichus a thousand drachmas and forbade further performances of the drama. Phrynichus, however, not to be deterred from his venture, composed a drama on the Persian wars called the *Phoenissae*. It had considerable success, as may be seen from the fact that the famous ode of the maidens in the play was a favorite among the older men in the Peloponnesian war.[27] Aeschylus, following the example of Phrynichus, composed the historical drama called the *Persians*. It was a success and has always been popular. In the *Eumenides*, dealing with the establishment of the Areopagus as a homicide court, some have seen propaganda against the efforts of Ephialtes and Pericles to deprive the Areopagus of its political functions.[28] Euripides in the Peloponnesian war did not hesitate to express anti-Spartan opinions, though he always put them into the mouths of heroic characters. But, apart from these experiments in historical and political drama, the mythological themes held their place.

We may suppose that the sentiment against making victories and defeats in Greek warfare the subject of treatment in art or the cause for the erection of any permanent memorial might well extend to the dramatic treatment of such themes. Under these circumstances, the historical drama would be confined to the Persian wars, which would soon be exhausted.

Mythology was safe and abundant, and soon had the sanction of tradition and appealed to religious conservatism. But it is little short of amazing that tragedy thus limited in themes should go on for two centuries producing new dramas, and continue to please the public. In large part this was due to the appeal which the singing of the chorus and the declamation of the actor had for an Athenian audience.[29]

It was inevitable that rhetoric should influence tragedy. "The older poets," says Aristotle,[30] "made their characters speak like citizens; the poets of the present day make them speak like rhetoricians." The change was already becoming manifest in Euripides, who composed long, balanced speeches in forensic style. This element in tragedy found favor with an audience which was so predisposed to oratory that it regarded even debates in the assembly somewhat in the nature of rhetorical contests. The fourth-century poets imitated the rhetorical element in Euripides. They were all trained by orators and some, like Theodectes, were orators as well as dramatists. But however monotonous and frigid such compositions must appear to modern taste, they continued to please the fourth-century audiences largely because of their rhetorical character.

Aeschylus, Sophocles, and Euripides were known as the "Three Tragic Poets" without mention of their names, though the names of Ion and Achaeus are found in the so-called canon of tragic poets.[31] The estimation in which they were held by the Athenian populace is shown by a decree

sponsored by Lycurgus, the orator (390-324 B.C.), requiring actors producing any of the plays of the three tragedians to refrain from rearranging or manipulating the
plays. To insure obedience of the law, the state secretary
was to attend performances with a copy drawn from the
state archives.[32]

Comedy was much more profoundly influenced in its development by democracy than was tragedy. Both forms of
the drama grew out of the worship of Dionysus. "Comedy
also," says Aristotle, "sprang from improvisations origi-
nating with the leaders of phallic ceremonies, which still
survive as institutions in many of our cities."[33] The purpose
of these phallic ceremonies was to insure fertility in man
and beast and earth. Indecency and obscenity were part
and parcel of these ceremonies, and were accepted by the
populace as a matter of course.[34] But the phallus was not
only a positive agent of fertilization, it was also a negative
charm against evil spirits. One of the most ancient methods
of driving off evil spirits is the use of abusive language. The
earliest fragments of Cratinus, the first comic poet whose
plays were preserved to later times, already exhibits the
most striking feature of fifth-century comedy, viz., its
"self-assumed censorship of the political and social life of
the period, coupled with daring in the use of invective, a
license in ridiculing institutions and persons, altogether
unexampled on the comic stage."[35] Ridicule and invective
found a ready acceptance in democratic Athens, so far as
they affected individuals. The Athenian attitude toward
comedy has been set forth very clearly by Pseudo-
Xenophon:[36]

Again they forbid ridicule and the abuse of democracy that they
may not hear ill of themselves, but they encourage it in individual cases, if anyone wishes to satirize another, well knowing
that the person satirized does not as a rule belong to the people
or the masses, but is either rich or well born or powerful; only

a few of the poorer classes and the democracy being ridiculed, and those only for officiousness and for seeking to advance themselves above the people, so that they do not object to men of that kind being ridiculed.

Nothing so clearly exhibits the nature of fifth-century Athenian comedy as the fact that the word κωμῳδεῖν must normally be translated by "ridicule," "satirize," "lampoon," "libel." The Greek language was well supplied with a vocabulary of vituperation, and the literature, from Homer on, shows that there was no hesitation in employing it with the full sanction of public opinion. It is evident from the passage just quoted that the utmost license in abuse was allowed on the stage, provided the government was not openly attacked. Such seems to be the interpretation of the words, "They do not permit ridicule and abuse of democracy on the stage."

The only recorded prosecution of a comedian is that of Aristophanes, as described in the *Acharnians*:[37]

> Aye and I know what I myself endured
> At Cleon's hands for last year's comedy,
> How to the council house he haled me off,
> And slanged and lied and slandered, and betongued me,
> Roaring Niagara-wise; till I well nigh
> Was done to death.

According to the scholiast, Cleon impeached him as a public offender because in the *Babylonians* he had attacked the Athenian magistrates and Cleon himself for misgovernment of the subject states of the empire. The offense was aggravated by the fact that the comedy was presented at the City Dionysia, to which allies, subjects, and strangers resorted in large numbers. But neither these lines from the *Acharnians*, nor the passage cited from Pseudo-Xenophon, prove that there was a specific law restricting freedom of speech on the comic stage at this time.[38] Cleon's choice of impeachment, instead of an ordinary criminal indictment, indicates pretty certainly that there was no specific law restricting freedom of speech in the theater. Impeachment in the fifth century was reserved for certain high crimes and misdemeanors and public offenses not included in the criminal code, which a legislator could neither forestall nor define.

The proceedings against Aristophanes before the council drew a goodly crowd that hoped to be amused by the witty rejoinders of the famous comedian under fire. The result of the trial is unknown. At most, a small fine may have been inflicted.[39] Aristophanes took the lesson to heart and observed more caution in the future. Later in the *Acharnians* Dicaeopolis, the hero of the play, undertakes to show that the Spartans were not altogether to blame for the war:[40]

> And I shall tell you startling things but true.
> Nor can Cleon slander me because,
> With strangers present, I defame the state.
> 'Tis the Lenaea, and we're all alone:
> No strangers yet have come; nor from the states
> Have yet arrived the tribute and allies.

To the same effect is his protest later in the play, that he is not criticizing the state but a lot of worthless citizens, the notorious sycophants.[41] So far as is known, Aristophanes escaped further molestation. There are references to restrictive measures adopted by the people on two different occasions, but they proved futile and short-lived. The reader of the comedies of Aristophanes and the fifth-century comic fragments is justified in concluding that if full license in speech was to be found anywhere in Athens it was on the comic stage.

For a long time comedies were presented at the Dionysiac festivals by volunteers without state subventions or patronage. This situation would seem to indicate that comedy was popular with the masses. It is not likely that volun-

teers would continue to put on comedies unless their performances met with popular approval. The first official
appearance of comedies was at the Dionysia in 486 B.C.,
the year after the introduction of the lot in the selection of
magistrates.[42] The date is significant. It can hardly be a
coincidence that a popular form of the drama was given
official support just after democracy had signalized its
growing power by substituting the lot for the ballot in selecting the archons. In 442 the state assumed responsibility
for the presentation of comedies at the Lenaea.[43] This was
the year in which Thucydides was ostracized. Henceforth,
Pericles' leadership was unchallenged. It was a fitting time
to add comedy to the Lenaea, at once enriching the festival
and gratifying the populace to whom Pericles owed his
victory.

Comedy was not, like tragedy, limited to any particular
type of theme. The plays of Aristophanes and the titles and
fragments of numerous other comedies exhibit the widest
possible range of subjects. But, owing to the importance of
Aristophanes and his predilection for political topics, the
old comedy, as it was called, is fittingly described as political. Still Aristophanes did not by any means confine himself to purely political themes such as peace, imperialism,
demagogues, and the jury system. Other topics, such as the
"new education" in the *Clouds*, communism in the *Parliament of Women* and the *Plutus*, and literary criticism in the
Frogs and *Thesmophoriazusae*, show the wide range of
themes that found favor with the Athenian populace. They
were practical subjects treated from the conservative standpoint with ridicule, satire, and never-failing good humor.
It is the great merit of Aristophanes that he could make
reforms appear ridiculous. His successors have found it
easier to hold up conservatism to ridicule.

A striking feature of old comedy is the constant exploitation of current tragic drama as a source of amusement.

Not only were scenes from tragedies burlesqued, but passages and even single lines were parodied. Aristophanes even went so far as to venture to interest and amuse his audience by a more or less detailed criticism of the works of Aeschylus and Euripides in the *Frogs*. That his efforts met with a large measure of success is shown by the fact that the comedy was awarded second prize. In the *Thesmophoriazusae* most amusing burlesques of scenes from Euripides' *Perseus* and *Andromeda* are introduced. And everywhere parodies and echoes of current tragedies occur and recur. "The extant plays are fairly sprinkled with pathetic lines and touching situations from tragedy, so distorted and put to uses so obviously incongruous as to be irresistibly funny even to the modern reader."[44] It is evident that the Athenians were very familiar with current tragedy. A comedian, striving to amuse his audience and gain a prize, would scarcely have ventured to make such use of the tragedians without being convinced that many would recall literally the original passages and lines. Hearers have better memories than readers. Even if one failed to recall the tragic lines that were parodied, the familiar diction and meter of tragedy, solemnly introduced upon the comic stage, was highly amusing by its very incongruity.

The popularity of Euripides is well attested in a well-known passage in Plutarch,[45] where it is related how many of the unfortunate survivors of the Sicilian expedition in 413 B.C. won their freedom by teaching what they could remember of the dramas of Euripides. Others found favor by reciting snatches of his lyrics.

Aristophanes seasoned his comedies with the frank indecencies that were the natural heritage of the ancient phallic rites and the Dionysiac *comus*. But he made an effort to raise the standard of the comic stage. In the *Clouds* (423 B.C.), he inveighed against slapstick comedy with its poor jokes, lascivious dances, and other vulgar characteristics that found favor with the audiences. In the *Peace*[46] (421 B.C.) he boasted that he had effected some reforms. Doubtless there is much truth in his claim if we may rely upon his description of the current practices on the comic stage, where Hercules was represented as a buffoon, "needy and seedy and greedy, a vagabond sturdy and stout, now baking his bread, now swindling instead, now beaten and battered about," or where a slave rushes in crying as a result of a beating, to give occasion for variations on an ancient pun on "flanks" as a military and anatomical term.

> Such vulgar contemptible lumber at once he bade from the drama depart,
> And then like an edifice stately and grand, he raised and ennobled the art.

There is evidence, however, that on occasion he yielded to the popular demand for vulgarity and buffoonery. The *Clouds* (423 B.C.) and the *Birds* (414 B.C.), two of his finest efforts according to modern standards of taste, both failed to receive first prizes because Aristophanes eschewed some of the time-honored devices that never failed to raise a laugh,[47] and ended with a real climax instead of the usual scene of boisterous revelry. But it is significant that in the *Wasps* (422 B.C.), which immediately succeeded the *Clouds*, he resorted to the discarded devices. The *Wasps* is a fine comedy, in which Aristophanes points out the political evils of the democratic jury system, but when the play is apparently ended by the regeneration of the old dicast, who is now content to hold domestic court for offenses committed in his household, a series of remarkable scenes is introduced. The old man goes out to a banquet, tells some trivial stories, gets drunk, and assaults various and sundry wayfarers as he wends his way homeward. The play ends with a grotesque dance, in which the old dicast joins some professional dancers whom he has challenged to a contest. There can be little doubt that we have here a deliberate, if unwilling, attempt to win public approval by conforming to the practices of which the dramatist had disapproved.

Attic comedy has been characterized as "dramatized debate." This characterization is largely justified by the emphasis laid upon the *agon* or debate between individual representatives of two opposing principles. A familiar *agon* in Aristophanes is the contest between the old and the new education as represented by the just and the unjust arguments in the *Clouds*. The question at issue is regularly settled by the chorus, or, as in the *Clouds*, by an individual, Pheidippides, the prospective student in the school of Socrates where the new plan of education is in vogue. It is true that the *agon* is not the product of sophistic rhetoric, for it is found, for instance, in the mimes of the Sicilian poet Epicharmus, who flourished before the development of rhetoric.[48] But it could not have occupied so prominent a place in comedy without the approval of a public actively interested in politics and accustomed to argument, discussion, and debate, as were the Athenians under democracy.

The dialogue was another type of literature which flourished in democratic Athens. The beginnings of the dialogue are found in the epic, and it was always an important element in the drama. As tragedy developed, there was a marked tendency to substitute lively and brief dialogue for the choral melodies that characterized the tragedies of Aeschylus. The full development of dialogue is found in Sophocles and Euripides. Hirzel[49] finds traces of dialogue in oratory. But dialogue could find no real place in oratory. The reproduction of conversations in a forensic speech is done rather from a desire to give a dramatic touch to the incident related. It is the same instinct which leads a Greek writer to drop naturally into direct discourse where the Roman adopts the indirect form.

The sophists made use of the dialogue in their instruction.[50] But Plato was the first to teach the real significance of the dialogue as the proper medium of dialectic. In his hands it ceased to be a rhetorical show piece and became an instrument of science and philosophy. After him no writer could participate in, or picture, the informal arguments, discussions, disputes, and debates of the period known as the Sophistic Illumination without imitating or reproducing them in the form of dialogues. Socrates made no speeches and wrote no books; his words could only be reproduced in dialogues. In the *Phaedrus*, Plato represents Socrates as objecting to the written word because a book cannot answer questions, meet objections, or correct misunderstandings.[51] Now, in a sense, the dialogue meets these objections in form at least. It has been well said that the dialogue is a "frozen conversation,"[52] for the interlocutors in a dialogue are represented as asking questions and obtaining answers, explanations, and corrections. The reader may not be satisfied with the answers, but there is some gratification in reading a book whose author understands that his thesis will meet with questions, disagreements, and misunderstandings. These features of the dialogue make it superior to the arguments of an essay or an exposition of a published speech as a means of publication among a people habituated and accustomed to oral interchange of thought on all occasions.

The influence of democracy upon the dialogue as a form of literature is not so obvious as upon oratory and the drama. But the intellectual background and basis of the dialogue is found in the general interest and participation in argument, discussion, and debate which is characteristic of Athenian democracy. This method of handling problems, whether in governing bodies or in the *agora*, the shops, or the *gymnasia*, depends upon the freedom of speech which democracy permitted and the general intelligence which it fostered.

Epistolography is closely related to the dialogue. A letter is a monologue or a half-dialogue in which a theme is developed.[53] As it is addressed to an individual, it is more lively than an essay and possesses a human interest involving both the writer and the receiver. In the collection known as *Epistolographi Graeci*, there are some letters purporting to belong to the fifth and fourth centuries; but with the possible exception of some attributed to Plato and Isocrates, they are generally regarded as spurious. Isocrates, in his letter to Dionysius of Syracuse, deliberately chose a letter in preference to a rhetorical composition addressed to a great festival. This and the letter to Archidamus, king of Sparta, have many similarities to the modern letter addressed to a particular individual but published also in the public press, because they have a preëminent public interest. But these letters did not become models for the development of a new type of literary expression. It was not until later that letter-writing came into vogue for various purposes, both personal and literary. In character, letters are rhetorical. The epistle did not escape the attention of the rhetoricians,[54] who formulated elaborate rules for composing different kinds of letters.

In conclusion, one may seriously inquire whether the literary history of Athenian democracy, particularly in drama and oratory, does not support the view of Aristotle[55] that "the many are better judges of music and poetry than a single individual."

CHAPTER VII

RELIGION

In Greece there was no hierarchy or organized priesthood to dominate, or interfere with, the government. Yet there was always a close relation between church and state. In the Heroic Age the king was religious head of the state. For certain kinds of sacrifice a priest was required.[1] Seers and prophets were men with certain gifts that gave them great power in the community, even under a monarchy. Chalcas was able to insist upon the sacrifice of Iphigenia, daughter of Agamemnon, commander-in-chief of the Grecian expedition against Troy, in spite of royal opposition. In matters of religion it is often dangerous to oppose a holy man when he is popularly regarded as the mouthpiece of the gods. But so long as Chalcas and his kind could not organize themselves and gain control of the cults and temples of the land, the civil power was secure.

In Athens there were a few hereditary priesthoods, in old family cults that had been taken over by the state, but otherwise the priests were selected and appointed by the government. Each shrine was independent of the others and had its own rules and ritual. Ordinarily the requirements of the priesthood were simple. Priests must be of citizen parentage and without physical blemish. The rule that men served gods and women served goddesses was not always followed. Occasionally celibacy was required for both priest and priestess during the term of office. In Athens the usual method of selection was by lot from a number of approved candidates.

The unification of Attica, which made Athens the largest territorial state in Hellas, was helped by the absorption of

local cults by Athens. Sometimes a local cult had a branch
in Athens. For example, the cult of Artemis at Brauron in
Attica had a branch on the Acropolis. Every fourth year a
procession went from Athens to Brauron. When Athens
incorporated Eleusis, the Eleusinian mysteries were celebrated by Athens. And Dionysus was brought to Athens
when Eleutherae was annexed. Hence the name Dionysus
Eleuthereus. The cult of Apollo was developed along the
east coast of Attica. Even after the sacred mission to Delos
was sent by Athens, the ship still sailed from Prasiae and
not from the Piraeus.

The process of unification must sometimes have encoun-
tered opposition in the tendency of the smaller communities to gravitate together for religious purposes, such as
Tetrapolis, or Four Towns, in the Marathonian region, but
as a rule religion served the cause of unification. These
adoptions and transfers of local cults set the seal of religion
upon the political unification of Attica. Henceforth, there
was one Prytaneum or state hearth for all Attica.[2] The
union of church and state was consummated. When the
aristocracy overthrew the monarchy, the royal powers were
distributed among the elective magistrates. All had some
religious duties, but one retained the royal title and became
the religious head of the state. He was known as the *archon
basileus*, or king archon.

In Attica the cults were originally in the hands of the old
aristocratic families. Evidence for this is found in the fact
that in Athens in later times certain priesthoods were hereditary in particular families. This means that the state took
over a highly developed private cult and made it accessible
to all, but left the charge of it in the hands of the family
that had originated it. Thus the family of the Boutidae
supplied the priestess for Athena Polias and the priest of
Poseidon-Erechtheus. Another proof of the privileged position of the nobility in the matter of religion is the fact

that the *exegetae*, or official expounders of the sacred law, were always members of the nobility.[3] The populace at large had no share in these cults except at the will of the nobility. The struggle for assured participation in the cults was part and parcel of the struggle for political privileges.[4] Solon did not face the problem of religious privileges for the masses directly, although his regulation of funeral rites was in the interest of democracy. It hindered the development of the cult of the grave, in which the populace could not participate.

In theory, the ancient city-state consisted of descendants from a common ancestor. Before the populace had full religious rights, the basis of the state was the phratries or brotherhoods. A phratry was composed of a noble family in all its branches, and such dependents and outsiders as it cared to admit into its ranks. At some time during the democratization of the state the phratries were required to admit outsiders. And so eventually every citizen was a member of a phratry. This regulation belongs to the reforms of Cleisthenes. Aristotle,[5] in his discussion of the means for preserving democracy, mentions with approval

measures like those which Cleisthenes passed when he wanted to increase the power of the democracy at Athens, or such as were taken by the founders of the popular government at Cyrene. . . . Fresh tribes and brotherhoods should be established; the private rites of families should be restricted and converted into public ones; in short, every contrivance should be adopted which will mingle the citizens with one another and get rid of old connections.

This measure of Cleisthenes made religion democratic. It was no longer in the hands of the aristocracy.

The rules and regulations governing admission of children and new citizens into the democratized phratries differed widely. But as a rule young children were introduced at the festival called Apaturia, which was celebrated in the latter part of October, the Athenian Pyanepsion. On intro-

ducing a child, the father, or his representatives, made an
oath that the child was his legitimate offspring by a law-
fully wedded wife, and offered a sacrifice of a sheep or a
goat with wine and bread. All the phratry members shared
in the feast. If it was decided that the child was entitled to
membership, he was duly enrolled in the phratry list,
called either κοινὸν γραμματεῖον or φρατερικὸν γραμματεῖον.
The Apaturia was so firmly associated with the registration
of children in the phratries that it became a recognized
family festival. All members of the family were expected
to be present and to participate in the festivities.[6]

For practical purposes the registration in a phratry established the right of children to inherit their father's property.[7] Girls, as well as boys, were registered as the lawful
children of a citizen. This was important. It was often difficult to prove that a woman was an Athenian, as required
by the citizenship law. In one legal case[8] phratry members
were introduced as witnesses to prove that a girl had not
been registered. In another case[9] it was asked why phratry
members were not brought in to prove that a certain woman was married to the man whose estate was in litigation.

Religion was associated with all public functions. Meetings of the assembly were opened with purificatory sacrifices and prayers. The herald pronounced curses against
those who should deceive the people in their speeches. If
any unfavorable omen such as thunder, lightning, an eclipse,
or an earthquake occurred, meetings were forthwith dissolved. In case of doubt the *exegetae* decided. In two assembly meetings of each prytany, provision was made for dealing with matters touching religion.[10] Decrees of the assembly
inscribed on stone slabs frequently have the word θεοί at
the top, as an appeal for the blessing of heaven upon their
deliberations. All officials were sworn in on assuming office.
Treaties were confirmed by oaths of the representatives
of the state.

The public religious festivals were managed by secular officials selected as other officials were. Cults could be changed and modified only by action of the assembly. New cults were readily enough accepted, though they could not be introduced without authorization of the civil powers. It was largely a question of finance. Festivals and shrines cost money. The festivals were normally civic or state affairs; but four—the Olympian, the Pythian, the Isthmian, and the Nemean—were recognized as national or Panhellenic. Athens was famous for the number and splendor of her state festivals. A fifth-century writer[11] tells us that Athens celebrated twice as many as any other Hellenic city. Their splendor is attested by Plato.[12] In the *Funeral Oration*, Pericles[13] says, "We have provided for the spirit many relaxations from toil; we have games and sacrifices regularly throughout the year." It has been estimated that about seventy days out of each year were given over to these religious festivals. Compared with our Sundays and other legal holidays amounting to at least sixty in all, this does not seem excessive. But the notorious congestion of public business in Athens was attributed in part to the religious festivals, during which no public body convened. They were very unevenly distributed throughout the year and often occupied several days each. The great Panathenaea was spread over six to nine days. This feature of Athenian holidays caused a more serious interruption to business than our better distributed holidays.

The Greeks regarded these celebrations as periods of rest and relaxation.

The gods [says Plato][14], in pity for the human race born to trouble, have ordained the feasts of thanksgiving as periods of respite from their trouble; and they have granted them as companions in their feasts the Muses and Apollo, the master of music, and Dionysus, that they may at least set right their modes of discipline by associating with the gods.

The festivals were managed and financed by the state. It was a definite policy of democracy to develop and enhance these celebrations, partly to impress allies and other visitors, but mainly for the gratification of the populace.

As for sacrifices and festivals [says Pseudo-Xenophon],[15] and shrines and consecrated enclosures, the people, knowing that it is not possible for the poor as individuals to sacrifice and make good cheer, and establish shrines and live in a great and beautiful city, have devised means to these ends; the city sacrifices a quantity of victims at the public expense, and it is the people which feasts and divides the victims by lot.

The democracy was ever ready to expand and embellish these festivals. For example, there is extant a decree of 421–420 making provision for raising the festival in honor of Hephaestus to the level of the Prometheus celebration by the addition of musical and gymnastic features to the original torch race.[16]

Athena, who was adopted as the patron goddess of Athens, appears in a Mycenaean painting as carrying a shield. In the *Odyssey*[17] she is represented as retiring to the stronghold of King Erechtheus in Athens. From this circumstance it has been inferred that Athena was originally, in Mycenaean times, the household goddess of the king, who had his residence on the Acropolis.[18] As the goddess of a warlike people, she was invested with a shield. When monarchy disappeared in Athens, Athena had already been adopted as the national divinity, and dwelt in a temple instead of the palace. It is significant that the name of the city is the plural of the name of the goddess. The Panathenaea was the greatest of the festivals in honor of Athena. It is probably as ancient as the cult of the goddess in Athens. Originally it was called "Athenaea," but after the unification of Attica it was enlarged and called "Panathenaea" to commemorate the event.[19] There was also instituted at the same time a special commemorative festival in honor of Athena variously known as ξυνοικία, συνοικεσία and μετοικία.

Pisistratus, the tyrant, established the more splendid Greater Panathenaea, the quadrennial celebration, which was so called because it embodied more features. Among them, in all probability, was the provision for the recitation of the poems of Homer. This theory is based upon the fact that at Brauron, the home of the Philiadae, to which family Pisistratus belonged, there was a contest of rhapsodists reciting the poems of Homer.[20] Musical features were added to the celebration of both the greater and the regular Panathenaea by Pericles. For the accommodation of the audiences at the musical contests, Pericles had the Odeon built. As the home of Athena, the Parthenon, begun under Themistocles, was finished in 438 under the influence of Pericles. In it stood the glorious chryselephantine statue of Athena in full armor. It was the work of Pheidias, one of the greatest of Greek sculptors. The frieze pictures the chief features of the procession that went up to the Acropolis to present a new *peplos* to Athena. There were other marks of honor and gratitude to their patron goddess that the Athenians constructed at this time. Among them was the little temple to Athena Nike, goddess of victory, built south of the entrance to the Acropolis. There was also a colossal bronze statue of Athena the Defender. Her gleaming helmet and spear-tip could be seen far out at sea.

The Panathenaea under democracy became a victory festival of the state goddess; but it was by no means a martial show. It always remained a religious celebration. The more important parts of the procession are represented on the frieze of the Parthenon. Metics or resident aliens had some part in the rites, but only Athenian participants are depicted on the frieze. At the end of the procession there was a sacrifice or hecatomb of oxen, to which the towns of

Attica and the colonies contributed. Hence there was abundance of meat, and the whole city and all accredited representatives feasted.

Equally important in the ritual was the presentation of the *peplos* to Athena. It was a saffron-colored robe on which were depicted the deeds of Athena as one of the Olympian gods. The priestess of Athena superintended the making of the garment. Athenian matrons and maids assisted. The chief honor fell to two maidens selected by lot from four elected from noble families. Here is another indication that religion was not entirely democratized. The age ranged from seven to eleven. Their functions in the making of the *peplos* were more or less ritualistic. In the procession they appeared beautifully clad and adorned with golden ornaments. Among the honors upon which Lysistrata prides herself was being chosen at seven to officiate as *arrephoros*, "bearer of the mystic casket"[21] in the Panathenaic procession. All the matrons and maidens were honored with crowns.

The whole festival was under the direct supervision of the *hieropoioi* chosen by lot, ten from the dicasts and ten from the council. Ten commissioners of games were selected by lot to manage the procession, the contests in music and gymnastics, and the horse race.[22] They held office for four years. Other secular officials participating in the celebration were the *archon eponymus* and the *archon basileus*.

With this glorious Athenian offering of sacrifice to Athena one naturally contrasts that earliest recorded offering of the *peplos* in ancient Troy.[23] The Trojans were being hard-pressed by the onslaughts of Diomedes. Hector repaired to the city and as the women surrounded him, inquiring eagerly about their men-folk, he urged them all to prayer. But he directed Hecuba, his mother, to select her most beautiful and precious *peplos* and, accompanied by all the noblest-born matrons of the city, to offer it to Athena in her temple and pray her to stay the hand of Diomedes. Here is no gala cult procession of happy people, but a solemn religious rite performed by women anxious for the safety of their city and of their men-folk. But vain was their prayer. Pallas Athena nodded in denial.

The holiday spirit seems to have pervaded these great religio-social gatherings.[24] There was no visible indication of religious exaltation or spiritual satisfaction such as is found in Christian religious services. For the Athenian every sacrifice was a feast, and in the Panathenaea the number of animals sacrificed was sufficient to give a sumptuous feast to those in charge of the celebration, and a meal to all. Strepsiades in the *Clouds* refers to the discomfort he suffered on one occasion by over-indulgence in Panathenaic stew. It is on such an occasion that Strepsiades says he had his face spattered with hot gravy while cooking the paunch of a sheep, which he had sacrificed with his relatives at the Diasia. Traders and hucksters of all kinds took advantage of these holiday gatherings to drive their trade. It was at one of these festival fairs that Strepsiades reminds his undutiful son that he bought him a toy cart when he was a little lad of six years.

Of an entirely different character were the famous Eleusinian Mysteries. There were processions and sacrifices as in the other rituals, but there was present a spiritual element which is lacking in the festivals of Athena and Dionysus. The rites and ceremonies of Eleusis were open only to persons who were duly initiated. Initiation required something more than a year for its completion. The fact that the *hierophant*, the chief religious official, was always one of the Eumolpidae, has led to the theory that Eumolpus established the Eleusinia. Other officials also, such as the heralds and the torch-bearers, belonged to certain families. The admission of slaves to initiation points to an original family cult. Some time in the sixth century it was taken over by the state. Pericles later endeavored to make it a great Panhellenic festival in the interest of Athenian imperialism.[25]

The Eleusinian ceremonies began in Athens, where the *mystae* assembled and bathed in the sea to purify themselves. There was a procession to Eleusis. When they had arrived there, they fasted and wandered about the sacred place in the early hours of darkness. Then they met in the great hall where they broke their fast, and the initiation was completed. The hierophant displayed the sacred objects; and the sacred drama, dealing with the experiences of Demeter and Kore, was performed on successive nights. Games and theatrical performances followed. On the return to Athens the king archon made a report of the celebration to the council. In this way state control was maintained.

The Mysteries had a personal appeal for the initiates that no other cult had. The fasting, the wandering about the sacred precinct, and the sight of the sacred objects in the lighted hall induced a spiritual exaltation and religious excitement that made the ceremonies very effective. There was no dogma or doctrine taught to the initiates, but vague hopes of well-being in this world and after death were aroused by the relationship established with divinities of the lower world. Pindar voices the personal satisfaction afforded by the Mysteries in the words: "Blessed is he who, having seen the mysteries, passes beneath the hollow earth."

The great popular interest in the Mysteries is shown by the fact that Alcibiades, who was sentenced to death *in absentia* for his alleged profanation of the Mysteries, signalized his return from banishment in 407 B.C. by celebrating the Mysteries in Eleusis under the protection of a military guard. Ever since the establishment of the enemy fortress at Decelea in Attica, the participants in the Mysteries had been transported by sea to Eleusis. Now for the first time in seven years the procession by land was re-

sumed in full pomp and splendor, and protected from molestation by the Spartan garrison in Decelea. Besides gratifying the religious feelings of the Athenians, Alcibiades
made his peace with the Eumolpidae and the Two Goddesses on whose account he had been condemned.[26]

The Eleusinian Mysteries filled the votaries with blessed
hope of wellbeing both here and hereafter; but the health
cults brought to their votaries no mere vague hopes, but
actual cures of bodily ills of every kind. One of the most
famous health cults was that of Asclepius, a demigod associated with the healing art. From Epidaurus, his most famous sanctuary, the cult spread to other cities. It was
introduced into Athens in 420-19 B.C., when democracy
was at its height.[27] But it was well known before that date.
In the *Wasps*[28] of Aristophanes the old man who has a mad
desire for spending his days in the courts as a dicast, is
represented as being taken to Ægina, where there was a
shrine of Asclepius, in the hope of curing his madness.

The patient slept in the precinct of the god. Sometimes
the cure took the form of a dream interpreted by the priest.
The interpretation was in the nature of a prescription. But
usually the affected part was touched in a vision by a
sacred animal, often a snake, and the patient awoke in the
morning cured. In the *Plutus* of Aristophanes there is an
amusing and instructive burlesque of the experiences of
the patients as they spent the night in the portico of the
sanctuary of Asclepius in Athens. The miracle of healing
performed on that occasion was the restoration of sight to
Plutus, the god of wealth. When his sight is restored, Plutus
proceeds to redistribute property according to people's
deserts, with amusing results.

The cock was a common offering to Asclepius. In the
Phaedo,[29] Socrates in his ironic manner reminds Crito, on
taking leave of him, that he owes a cock to Asclepius, and
asks him not to forget it. The offering was to express his

gratitude for being cured of a great malady—life—by the draught of hemlock.

The cult of Asclepius is more intelligible to the modern world than is any of the other ancient religious rites and ceremonies. Scores of healing cults flourish among us. Their votaries are found everywhere in every stage of society.[30] While these modern cults differ widely from the ancient cult of Asclepius, there remains enough in common to enable us to understand his worshipers. To them, religion brought substantial benefits in the shape of cures.

Strabo,[31] the geographer, says, "Epidaurus is distinguished on account of the manifestations of Asclepius there, who is believed to cure all manner of diseases, and whose sanctuary is always full of sick people, and of votive tablets recording the cures." Modern excavators have found ample confirmation of the statement of Strabo in a record of some twenty cures of suppliants. Two of these "cures of Apollo and Asclepius," as they were called, are worth quoting.

Ambrosia of Athens, blind of an eye. She came as a suppliant to the god, but walking around the sanctuary she scoffed at some of the cures as incredible and impossible, that the halt and the blind should be made whole by merely seeing a vision in their sleep. But she in her sleep saw a vision. It seemed that the god stood over her and announced that he would cure her of her disease, but that by way of payment she would have to present to the sanctuary a pig made of silver as a memento of her ignorance. And when he had thus said, he cut open her diseased eye and poured in a healing drug, and when the day dawned she went away cured.

And again,

A man's toe was healed by the serpent. This man, suffering grievously in his toe by a malignant ulcer, was brought forth while it was yet day by the attendant and took his seat on a bench. When he had fallen asleep, a serpent issued out of the temple and licked it; and when he awoke, healed, he said that he had seen a vision: it seemed as though a youth of comely appearance had laid upon his toe a healing drug.[32]

It may be noted that there is no question here of a sect or body of initiates to which the suppliant must belong. There was no creed or dogma to which he must subscribe. All were welcome. Even scoffers were cured.

Apart from the state festivals and cults, the religion of the normal Athenian centered in the home and the phratry. The head of a family himself performed the rites for the family at the hearth without the intervention of a priest. When animals were killed for food a portion was sacrificed. Sometimes guests were invited to share. The after-dinner symposium always began with a libation. On all sorts of occasions prayers, sacrifices, and libations were offered. So fixed were the religious usages of daily life that Socrates,[33] when handed the death draught, inquired if a part might be used for libation.

The most distinguished public buildings in Athens—the temples on the Acropolis, the Odeon, and the theater of Dionysus—were intimately associated with religion. The same is true of sculpture during its earlier period. Indeed, without religion, neither architecture nor sculpture could have developed and flourished as they did. The Persian occupation of Athens left its buildings in ruins and the crude images of the gods broken and destroyed. Athens was the chief, but not the sole, sufferer from the depredations of Persia. One of the professed objects of the Delian league was to obtain reparations from Persia for war damages.[34] This purpose was only partly successful. But as the league grew into an Athenian empire and the danger from Persia diminished, Pericles conceived the idea of using the surplus tribute in beautifying Athens with temples and sculpture. The conservatives, led by Thucydides, opposed the plan. Democracy supported Pericles and ostracized Thucydides in 443 B.C. The argument of Pericles that, since Athens suffered most from Persia, it was only right that the allies should contribute to the restoration of the religious monuments of the city, was calculated to associate religion with imperialism in the popular mind. But it must be admitted that the prospect of profit from the expenditure of so much money and the desire to have a beautiful city weighed heavily in favor of Pericles' policy. Before the end of the fifth century the Acropolis became the greatest artistic center in the ancient world. Xenophon reports Socrates as saying that the most suitable location for temples and altars was a conspicuous site remote from traffic, for "it is pleasant to utter a prayer as one gazes upon them and to approach them unsullied by human contacts." The temples on the Acropolis fulfilled these conditions admirably. They were visible from every part of the city, and accessible by a winding path that led only to the Acropolis.[35]

Apart from ceremonial uses the temple precincts and porticos served other purposes. Enemies who wished to reconcile their differences were accustomed to resort to these sacred places to render their agreements more solemn and binding.[36] Arbitrators also were in the habit of resorting to temples for their sittings.[37] Some of the homicide courts were established at shrines. But there is no evidence that the citizen ever entered the presence of the cult statue for contemplation and worship.

In a speech of Isaeus[38] there occurs a most interesting passage recording some of the religious activities of Ciron, an elderly Athenian of some means. Two young men, alleging that they were the grandsons of Ciron, claimed his estate. One of them spoke in court. To show that Ciron had always treated them as his grandsons he says:

As was natural, seeing we were sons of his own daughter, Ciron never offered a sacrifice without our presence; whether he was performing a great or a small sacrifice, we were always there and took part in the ceremony. And not only were we invited to such rites, but he always took us to the country for the Dionysia, and we always went with him to public spectacles. We went to his house to keep all the festivals; and when he sacrificed to Zeus Ctesius [guardian of the family property]—a festival to which he attached a special importance, and to which he admitted neither slaves nor free men outside his own family, and at which he performed all the rites—we participated in the celebration and laid our hands with his upon the victims and placed our offerings side by side with his, and took part in all the other rites, and he prayed for our health and wealth.

Both the state and the individual in ancient and primitive communities were deeply interested in gaining knowledge of the future. The means of reading the future were various. A common and widespread method of divination was by means of oracles. The individual could go to an oracular shrine and address his questions to the official servant of the god. The popularity of oracles in Hellas is indicated by the number of famous oracular shrines, such as Delphi, Dodona, Branchidae, Colophon, Lebadeia, and Oropus. Of these the most famous was Delphi. From Delphi came the oracle that, according to Socrates, motivated his life. Chaerephon, a friend and pupil of Socrates, had inquired of Apollo if any man was wiser than Socrates. The answer was, "No one is wiser than Socrates." When this reply was reported to Socrates, he doubted its truth and proceeded to test the oracle by questioning any and every person who had a reputation for wisdom. An investigation that had begun in curiosity became in the mind of Socrates a holy mission imposed upon him by the god to prove his infallibility. At the age of seventy he reported to the jury the conclusion he had reached, viz., that he was wiser than others because he "did not think he knew what he did not know."

In addition to the oracles given at the shrines in response to queries of worshipers, there were many collections of oracles and prophecies in the possession of states or individuals. These were consulted by state officials on occasion. A collection that went under the name of *Bacis* was well known in Athens, as we learn from Aristophanes. The Athenians were no more superstitious or credulous than other ancient peoples; but there was always a swarm of seers, soothsayers, prophets, and oracle-mongers abroad. The last-named produced oracles for all occasions, usually claiming that they came from a well-known collection. In times of national distress and danger the people turned eagerly to these charlatans. Thucydides remarks on the flood of prophecies set loose by the Peloponnesian war. When the Peloponnesians first invaded Attica the populace could scarcely be restrained from going forth to engage the foe. "They gathered in knots and engaged in hot disputes, some urging that they should go out, others opposing this course. Oracle-mongers were chanting oracles of every import, according as each man was disposed to hear them."[39]

An example of the political effect of oracles is found in the decision to undertake the Sicilian expedition in 415 B.C.There is no doubt that the activities of oracle-mongers strongly influenced public opinion in favor of it. And when they were informed of the destruction of the fleet and army in Syracuse, the Athenians specifically blamed the orators and the oracle-mongers."They were angry with the orators, who had taken part in promoting the expedition—as though they had not themselves voted for it—and they were also enraged at the oracle-mongers and soothsayers and whoever at that time by any practice of divination had led them to hope that they would conquer Sicily."[40]

Further evidence of the popular interest in oracles is found in the comedies of Aristophanes. An oracle motivates two plays, the *Knights* and the *Plutus*, while a scene in the *Birds* and one in the *Lysistrata* are motivated by oracles. In each the "oracles" are comic inventions, interpreted in the oracular manner by comic "chresmologists" or expounders of oracles.

One cannot but wonder if politicians may not, on occasion, have purposely circulated oracles to influence public opinion in favor of certain policies. In the *Knights* of Aristophanes there is the merest hint that Cleon used oracles in this fashion. Cleon, as a Paphlagonian slave, is represented as supplanting the other slaves in the favor of his master, the old man Demos, the personification of democracy. One of the slaves, representing Demosthenes, the general, who was the military genius in the final attack on the Spartans hemmed in on Sphacteria, voices this complaint: "He drives us away and allows none of us to pay court to the master, but with a leather swatter in his hand he stands beside him as he dines and flicks away the orators, *and he chants oracles, for the old man is keen on them.*"[41] Some samples of his oracles are given in the play. Cleon, in defense of his war policy, says that Demos will rule over all Hellas. "For the oracles say that some day Demos shall sit in judgment in Arcadia at five obols per day." This comic oracle reminds the audience that Cleon raised the dicasts' pay to three obols. There is also a reference to a favorite oracle about the eagle in the clouds, which may well have been used by speakers to flatter the people:

> O thou fortunate town
>   Of Athene, the bringer of spoil,
> Much shalt thou see, and much
>   Shalt thou suffer, and much shalt thou toil,
>
> Then in the clouds shalt thou soar, as an eagle for ever
>   and ever.[42]

In the contest of oracles between Cleon and Agoracritus in the play, there is a suggestion that politicians made some use of oracles in urging their policies, but the occasions on which they could do so effectively must have been few.[43]

There is, however, no indication that even in the discussions about the Sicilian expedition there was any coöperation between the orators and the oracle-mongers. Yet it is beyond question that, in a community where every citizen was a member of the governing body in the state, an appeal to popular superstition by means of oracles and prophecies in troublous times would immediately and inevitably be reflected to some extent in public measures. And such was the case in democratic Athens.

But a trip to Delphi or other famous shrines was not possible for all Athenians. Many resorted to other well-known means of divination, such as sacrifices, dreams, signs of nature, and, particularly, the flight of birds. In fact, so common was the practice of drawing omens from birds that *ornis*, "bird," is metaphorically used for "omen." Aristophanes, in his comedy entitled the *Birds*, enumerates the services of birds to humanity, giving prominence to their use as omens.

Thus your Ammon, Dodona, and Delphi are we; we are also your
    Phoebus Apollo.
For whatever you do, if a trade you pursue, or goods in the mar-
    ket are buying,
Or the wedding attend of a neighbor or friend, first you look to
    the Birds and their flying.
And whenever you of an omen or augury speak, " 'tis a bird,"
    you are always repeating.
A rumor's a bird, and a sneeze is a bird, and so is a word or a
    meeting,
A servant's a bird and an ass is a bird. It must therefore assuredly
    follow
That the birds are to you (I protest it is true) your prophetic
    divining Apollo.[44]

Pollution and purification were always prominent characteristics of ancient religions. Greek religion was no exception. As we have seen, trials for homicide were originated largely because the shedder of blood came to be regarded as polluted. The state intervened to protect the citizens from personal contamination by discovering and banishing the guilty one. Association with a murderer was regarded as a dangerous business. One might be involved in destruction with him by the wrath of the gods. The presence of a polluted person at a sacrifice would render it of no avail. The Athenians were so convinced of the reality of pollution and its potency for injury that one of Antiphon's clients,[45] who was defending himself against a charge of homicide, produced witnesses to show that his fellow-voyagers were never in danger from his presence on the ship, though it was well known that many men had lost their lives under similar conditions in the past. He proved also that his presence had never interfered with the favorable outcome of a sacrifice. The fear of pollution is further evidenced in the institution of the court of the Prytaneum to discover and cast beyond the border animals and inanimate objects that had caused the death of a human being.

With such conceptions of moral pollution imbedded in the religion of the Athenians, it is not strange that their public policy was not infrequently affected thereby. It was customary, when the city was in great danger and needed the support of all its citizens, to restore political rights to all who were suffering under disabilities of any kind. But when exiles were recalled under a decree of amnesty, there was a clause specifically excluding from the benefits of amnesty all exiles tainted with the pollution of blood-guiltiness.[46]

In Athens a celebrated case of pollution had some important political repercussions. In 632 B.C. Cylon attempted to make himself tyrant of Athens by force. Some of his followers, being besieged in the Acropolis and reduced by hunger to despair, took refuge in the temple of Athena Polias. On a promise that their lives would be spared they were induced to leave the temple, but were forthwith slain. Megacles, of the Alcmaeonid family, was archon. On a charge of sacrilege the Alcmaeonids and their friends, who had acted with them, were later condemned to perpetual exile and their property was confiscated.[47] After the expulsion of the Pisistratidae in 510 B.C. by the Spartans, the Alcmaeonids were restored; but the adherents of the tyrants, under the leadership of Isagoras, succeeded in enlisting the Spartans to "drive out the pollution" in the person of the restored Alcmaeonids. Cleisthenes, their leader, withdrew, and Cleomenes, the Spartan king, expelled seven hundred families as polluted. But the populace wanted no more of the tyrants, and soon Cleisthenes, the head of the Alcmaeonids, returned and became the second founder of democracy in Athens.

For two generations the matter was apparently forgotten. Then, on the eve of the Peloponnesian war, the question of the polluted Alcmaeonidae was raised by the Spartans. In the diplomatic jockeying that immediately preceded the outbreak of the war, the Spartans first sent an embassy to demand that the Athenians "drive out the curse of the goddess." As Thucydides explains, this was a demand to expel the descendants of Megacles, the Alcmaeonid who first polluted the city. The purpose was to embarrass Pericles. Pericles was at that time the most distinguished member of the Alcmaeonid family through his mother, a niece of Cleisthenes. He was also the ruling popular leader and a vigorous opponent of concessions to Sparta. The Spartans pretended that the demand was made in order to avenge the honor of the gods, but it was really aimed at Pericles. If he were banished, a remote possibility, they might hope to gain concessions from the Athenians, but in any event they expected to discredit Pericles in the eyes of the Athenians. The Athenian answer, dictated no doubt by Pericles, directed that Sparta cleanse her own city of pollution.[48]

Neither of the demands was taken seriously by either side. In the Athenian assembly which decided to reject the final Spartan demand to dissolve the empire by "letting the Hellenes go free," Pericles in his speech made no reference to the question of pollution. Perhaps as a good politician he took the wiser course in ignoring the matter. It is not again referred to by Thucydides.

A most serious disturbance in Athens was caused by a wholesale destruction of the crude busts of Hermes found throughout the city in large numbers, beside porticos, temples, and private houses, in the *agora*, at street intersections, and other conspicuous places.[49] The outrage occurred on the eve of the sailing of the armada to Sicily in 415 B.C. It stirred people beyond our imagination to realize, as subsequent events showed. Was it done by those who wished to stop the expedition? Was it done by enemy emissaries to bring down the wrath of heaven upon them? Was it a drunken prank of young men who in the contemporary enlightenment had lost most of their reverence for things sacred? Or was it a desperate deed devised to bind together conspirators against the democracy, a pledge of evil? These and other questions were asked throughout the city. Whatever the answer was, the deed was an insult to those heavenly powers that gave the Athenians aid and comfort. As usual in cases of impiety, the council, which was empowered to investigate the matter, encouraged the production of information regarding any other acts of impiety. It soon developed that Alcibiades was involved in a burlesque performance of mysteries in a private house. His enemies were afraid to bring to trial a general of the popular expedition while the soldiers and sailors were still in the city. For the moment he was allowed to depart, but within a short time he was recalled for trial. Realizing the dangerous state of mind of the people as the result of the shock to their religious sensibilities, he escaped and went to Sparta, where he did much harm to his native city by encouraging the Spartans to carry out the plan to build at once a fortress in Attica at Decelea. But Alcibiades was later recalled and made his peace with the Eleusinian divinities.[50] Within five years after the mutilation of the Hermae, Aristophanes jested about it on the comic stage.[51]

The Athenians took strange liberties with their gods on the comic stage, without fear of reproach or danger of impiety. They daily "took their names in vain" in asseverations and denials. Socrates' oaths by the "dog" and the "goose" are supposed to be protests against the general custom; but it was a mere gesture. Plato might protest against the immoral tales about the gods in myth and song, but he was a "voice and nothing else."

In matters of religion there were toleration and liberality. There was no compulsion to join in public religious ceremonies and rites and festivals. But a man could not dissociate himself from the family and tribal religious observances and the ceremonies attendant upon birth, death, and marriage without incurring intolerable reproach.

Liberal as democracy was, there was a limit to tolerance. About the last third of the fifth century, when democracy was firmly settled in power, there appears to have been a reaction. The spirit of inquiry was abroad. The new education supplied by the sophists who came from all parts of Hellas must have disturbed the old beliefs and superstitions, especially among the people of means. But in spite of the growing dissatisfaction with the traditional cosmogony, and the interest in speculations regarding physical forces as the causes of things in the heavens above or on the earth beneath, there was in the masses a very considerable suspicion of all this new thought. There was also a political element involved. Politicians did not hesitate to cast suspicion upon the orthodoxy of their opponents. Pericles, by his friendship with Anaxagoras, laid himself open to attack.[52]

In this atmosphere one Diopeithes supplemented whatever legal provisions against heterodoxy there were in the Solonian laws, by a decree "that impeachments should be brought against those persons who did not believe in the gods or taught doctrines regarding celestial phenomena."[53] Diopeithes was the butt of the comic poets for his fanaticism and his superstition. He disliked Anaxagoras and no doubt suspected Pericles because of his relations with him. The genuine old Athenians shared the views of Diopeithes in regard to Anaxagoras.[54] A scholiast says Diopeithes was a friend of Nicias, that staunchest of all orthodox Athenians of the late fifth century. The impeachment of Anaxagoras that followed the decree of Diopeithes is generally regarded as a blow at Pericles. This is doubtless true. In a democracy the wise politician refrains from arousing the religious sensibilities of the populace; the wily one plays up to them by taking a public stand on the side of orthodoxy.

There were other prosecutions for impiety in this period. Diagoras of Melos was prosecuted because he had expressed impious views on the Athenian public festivals. In the *Clouds*,[55] performed in 423, Aristophanes maliciously calls Socrates "the Melian," with the purpose of branding him as an atheist. About the same time Cleon prosecuted Euripides for impiety.[56] The prosecution seems to have failed. There is some significance in the fact that Cleon, a representative of the middle class, thus came out on the side of orthodoxy. He had learned rhetoric to some purpose, as his speeches in Thucydides show, but his attitude on the Mytilenean debate shows that he was reactionary and conservative to a fault, in comparison with his thoughtful and wise opponent Diodotus, who is otherwise unknown. But whether Cleon's orthodoxy was due to policy or conviction, it shows that the democracy of the Peloponnesian war era was not so liberal in religion as the earlier democracy had been. But no people are normal in war.

Socrates was not molested during this period. But come-
dians attacked him. In 423, he was derided by Ameipsias
in the *Connus* with a chorus of "professors" (φροντισταί).
It was thought even among the ancients[57] that the *Clouds*,
produced by Aristophanes in the same year, was intended
to rouse the public to the dangers of Socratic teaching.
And Socrates in his *Apology* refers to an unnamed comedian as the source of most of the prejudice against him.
Whether a prosecution was intended at that time and abandoned because of lack of public interest, is not known. It
seems likely, for the charges in the *Clouds*, if true, rendered
Socrates liable under the decree of Diopeithes. It was not
until twenty-four years later that Socrates was finally
brought to trial. Much had happened in the meantime.
There had been two revolutions. Socrates remained in
Athens during the rule of the Thirty Tyrants, whose leader,
Critias, had been his pupil. This was ground for suspicion.
Socrates did not go into exile, as did most of the democrats
who were not put to death. True it is that Critias forbade
Socrates to teach young men, and that Socrates defied the
orders of the Thirty to participate in the arrest of Leon of
Salamis. In his defense Socrates claimed that his defiance
would have cost him his life if the régime of the Thirty had
endured. However, the amnesty of 403 B.C. should have
afforded him protection against any sort of political prosecution. And it would seem that, as a result of measures
adopted by the restored democracy, the decree of Diopeithes,
under which the earlier prosecutions for impiety had been
conducted, was no longer in force. Socrates was tried in 399
for impiety. There was also a charge that he corrupted the
youth.[58] The relation between this charge and the general
indictment for impiety has given rise to much discussion.
Some believe that the corruption of the youth was an overt
act of impiety; others that offenses against public morality
could be attached to a general charge of impiety. It is dif-

ficult to reach a decision because the provisions of the law dealing with impiety are not known.

Another difficulty is that the speeches of the prosecutors of Socrates have not survived. Meletus, his chief accuser, was doubtless a fanatical champion of religion, as he prosecuted Andocides in the same year for impiety. On the face of it the prosecution was religious, but it has been suspected on good grounds that there was a fear abroad that Socrates was dangerous to the extreme democracy of the fourth century. But just how the prosecutors persuaded a jury of five hundred to convict him we shall probably never know, for the prosecutors' speeches are not extant, and the defense of Socrates as it appears in the *Apology* of Plato and the *Apology* of Xenophon is an uncertain source for reconstructing the lines of attack by the prosecutors. They are not real forensic speeches. Socrates rejected the offer of Lysias to provide him with a suitable speech; but in rejecting it Socrates was right, for not even an expert like Lysias could have done justice to a client like Socrates. He composed his own defense.

It seems reasonable to suppose that, quite apart from the rather vague charge of impiety, there was a political element in the trial of Socrates.[59] It is known that he held up to ridicule election by lot. Such criticism, combined with the suspicion created by his failure to go into exile with the loyal democrats during the régime of the Thirty, may very well have aroused doubts as to his loyalty to democracy. He had been the teacher of the notorious Alcibiades, and of Critias, the chief among the Thirty Tyrants. There could have been no fear that Socrates himself would take part in any anti-democratic conspiracy. But might his teachings not be a source of danger to the extreme form of democracy that developed after the restoration in 403?

When all is said and done, the condemnation and execution of Socrates for any cause, religious, moral, or political, is a blot on the fair name of Athens. It should, however, be pointed out in extenuation that in both ancient and modern times the opinion has prevailed that, had Socrates proposed banishment as a counter-penalty, a majority of the dicasts would have been satisfied; but instead he proposed a small fine, coupled with the assurance that he had no intention of mending his ways. This conduct was little short of a studied insult to the proudest public body in Athens. They had in their hands the means of gratifying their resentment, and a much larger majority voted for the death penalty demanded by the prosecutors. In a sense the blood of Socrates was on his own head.

Aristotle, speaking of democracy, says that "every contrivance should be adopted which will mingle the citizens with one another." At Athens the democratized phratries and cults were admirably fitted to mingle the citizens together. Religion had become socialized. At regular periods throughout the year the whole population, without distinction of birth or wealth, mingled together joyously in celebrating their splendid festivals and in honoring their national divinities.

To the modern world Athenian religion has left a substantial legacy in sculpture, in architecture, and in the dramatic literature which is still its greatest cultural heritage.

CHAPTER VIII

IMPERIALISM

THE PERSIANS were decisively defeated both by land and by sea in 480 and 479 B.C. But the Greeks fully realized that their only safety lay in expelling these enemies from the Ægean Islands and sea coast. For some time the Spartans led the allied forces in this campaign; but their leader, Pausanias, the victor at Plataea, became so unpopular with the other Greeks that they offered the leadership to the Athenians. The expulsion of the Persians from the Ægean was after all a matter of sea power, and in that the Athenians excelled. The Athenians accepted the task and formed the league known as the Confederacy of Delos, because that island was the meeting place of the league representatives. It was not chosen because of its convenience, but because it had long been the religious center of the Ionians, where they gathered to honor Apollo[1] with dance and song and games.

Pisistratus, the tyrant, in his policy of extending the power and influence of Athens, had purified the island and strengthened the claim of Athens to be the head of the Ionian branch of the Greek race. As the majority of the league was Ionian it was a wise policy to give the league a home in a sanctuary like other Amphictyones, or neighborhood associations. Athens was naturally the dominant partner in the league. Her generals and admirals commanded the military and naval forces of the league, and Athenian officials known as Hellenic treasurers[2] had charge of the funds, which were deposited in the temple of Apollo. Within a comparatively short time this voluntary association became the Athenian empire. For this change the allies were themselves largely responsible.

Most of the allies [says Thucydides],[3] on account of their aversion to military service, in order to avoid being away from home, got themselves rated in sums of money instead of ships, which they should pay in as their proportionate contributions, and consequently the fleet of the Athenians was increased by the funds which they contributed, while they themselves, whenever they revolted, entered the war without preparation and without experience.

At the end of a few decades there remained only three independent allies. The others were subjects of Athens.

Whatever advantages may have accrued to the Delian league from the religious associations of the island were forfeited entirely when the treasury was removed to Athens in 454. This step marks the formal establishment of the empire. Athens became an imperial city. The tribute was transferred from the keeping of Apollo to that of Athena, patron goddess of Athens, now the goddess of the empire.[4] For this service one-sixtieth of the tribute was dedicated to Athena each year. It also lent an air of sanctity to the collection of the tribute. The reason for the transfer was the danger to the treasury after the catastrophe of the Egyptian expedition, which for the time being left the Ægean exposed to the triumphant Phoenician fleet in the Persian service.

But Athens was not unmindful of the advantage of making full use of religion in forwarding her imperial policy. Some time between 445 B.C. and 431 B.C., a commission brought in a report regarding the offerings of the first-fruits of the harvest to the Eleusinian goddesses, an ancient ceremony which had been neglected and permitted to fall into disuse.[5] The commission recommended that the subject states be required to send in their contributions and that invitations be sent to other Greek states to participate in the offering. It seems that Athens intended that the rehabilitated Eleusinian mysteries should in some measure take the place of the Delian festival, and that the Eleusinian rites should be a great Hellenic festival under the patronage of imperial Athens.

This was not the only attempt made to link up the overseas subjects with the great state festivals. The tributary states were required to participate in the Panathenaea, a festival in honor of Athena.[6] It was a distinctly national festival, and participation in it was intended to emphasize the intimate relationship between Athens and her subordinate and allied cities, similar to that between a colony and the mother city. Other festivals, such as that of the Great Dionysia, were intended to show the greatness and splendor of Athens. Attendance of the citizens of the subject states at the celebration of the Dionysia was encouraged by the practice of receiving the annual tribute at this time. A sense of dependence and inferiority was naturally engendered by the sight of so many cities offering their tribute to the great imperial city, while the splendid temples, the great dramatic performances, and the evidences on every hand of wealth and power showed that they served no mean mistress.

To counteract the growing suspicions of the Lacedaemonians, who began to view with some concern the growth of Athenian power, Pericles proposed to summon the Greeks from all parts of Hellas, both in Europe and Asia, to a great convention at Athens to consider matters of common interest, in 450-49. They were as follows:

To consult and advise concerning the Greek temples which the barbarians had burned down, and the sacrifices which were due from them upon vows they had made to their gods for the safety of Greece when they fought against the barbarians; and also concerning the navigation of the sea, that they might henceforth pass to and fro and trade securely and be at peace among themselves.

Such is Plutarch's[6] account of a great project which came to nought. For the twenty ambassadors sent throughout

Hellas to persuade the cities to send delegates failed in their mission. One wonders if Pericles ever expected them to succeed. In any event, they must have done good service as propagandists.

Athens had suffered most from the Persian invasion so far as temples and shrines were concerned. To restore them might very well be represented as the duty of the Greeks. In any event, the use of the surplus funds derived from the tribute to restore them in splendid fashion could be justified as a matter of collective responsibility in their duty to the gods. It put the Periclean building program in a somewhat different light in the eyes of the Hellenes, even if it did not reconcile them to it. It was extraordinarily clever propaganda.

In Athens, in spite of opposition, Pericles was successful in carrying out his policy of building temples and beautifying Athens in such fashion that his opponents said that the city, like a vain woman, was being "decked out with precious stones and figures and temples."[7]

The economic aspect of imperialism appealed to the Athenian people as it did to all Greeks. An early suggestion of the financial advantages of turning the league into an empire came from Aristides, who, owing to his reputation for honesty and impartiality, had been entrusted with the task of making the first assessment of tribute.

Aristides, seeing the state growing in confidence and much wealth accumulated, advised the people to lay hold of the leadership of the league and quit the country districts and settle in the city. He pointed out to them that they would all be able to gain a living there, some by service in the army, others in the garrisons, others by taking a part in public affairs. . . . This advice was taken, and they secured an ample maintenance for the mass of the population. . . . Out of the proceeds of the tributes and the taxes and the contributions of the allies more than twenty thousand citizens received pay.[8]

Among these Aristotle lists seven hundred overseas officials who were doubtless engaged directly in the imperial administration. Litigation that originated in the empire must have given considerable employment to the six thousand dicasts, while the court fees swelled the general revenue. There was, furthermore, considerable recourse of citizens to the capital both for business and for sightseeing, particularly at the time when the festivals were celebrated. Such visitors spent appreciable sums of money during their sojourn. A fifth-century writer[9] has given examples of these expenditures. They consisted of harbor dues, rent of lodgings, hire of servants and beasts of burden, and fees of heralds and criers. This is by no means a complete list such as is compiled by agencies estimating the value of tourist trade nowadays. Such sojourners in Athens must have stimulated trade in many directions. But Athens did not leave the stimulation of trade and commerce in the empire wholly to chance. Evidence on the subject is meager, but enough is available to enable us to trace a very definite imperial commercial policy. To begin with, the Athenians possessed in the Piraeus one of the most favorably located ports in Greece. Xenophon, in his essay on *Revenues*,[10] enumerates the advantages and attractions of Athens as a center of commercial enterprise:

The city of Athens lies at the navel not of Greece merely but of the habitable world. . . . The traveler who desires to traverse the confines of Hellas from end to end will find that whether he voyages by sea or by land he is describing a circle the center of which is Athens. Once more this land, though not literally sea-girt, has all the advantages of being accessible to every wind that blows and can invite to its bosom or waft from its shores all products, since it is a peninsula; while by land it is the emporium of many markets as being a portion of the mainland. . . . We possess the finest and safest harborage for shipping, where vessels of all sorts can come to mooring and be laid up in absolute security so far as stress of weather is concerned. But further than that, in most states the trader is under the necessity of lading his vessel with some merchandise or other in exchange for his cargo, since the current coin has no circulation beyond the frontier. But at Athens he has a choice: he can, in return for his wares, either export a variety of goods, such as human beings seek after, or if he does not desire to do this he can simply export silver.

There is no doubt that the Athenians succeeded in building up a great port in the Piraeus. "Whatever desirable things," says another writer,[11] "are found in Sicily, Italy, Cyprus, Lydia, the Pontus, the Peloponnesus, or anywhere else, are all brought together at Athens on account of her mastery of the sea." In the Funeral Speech, Pericles[12] is represented as saying, "Our city is so great that all the products of all the earth flow in upon us, and ours is the happy lot to gather in the fruits of our own soil with no more home-felt security of enjoyment than we do those of other lands." This immense trade was fostered and secured in various ways.

The greatest menace to free commercial intercourse was piracy. In tracing the early commercial growth of Corinth, Thucydides[13] remarks: "When navigation grew more prevalent among the Hellenes, the Corinthians acquired ships and swept the sea of piracy, and offering a mart by sea as well as by land, raised their city to great power by means of their revenues." Naturally Athens also took measures to suppress piracy, which never wholly disappeared from the Mediterranean, and it was no doubt owing to her efforts that it practically disappeared from the main trade routes though it was still prevalent among the Locrians, Aetolians, Acarnanians, and others in that part of Greece. Various means were resorted to in the effort to render the sea routes safe. A naval power could always render pirate lairs untenable. Thus in 474 Cimon dispersed the Dolopian pirates from the island of Scyrus and settled Athenian colonists on the island.[14] In the fourth century the allies of the Athenians were induced to adopt preventive measures against pirates.[15] Evidently the local authorities were required to exclude robbers and pirates from their harbors. Failure to do so was punished by fines. In the fifth century, when all but three cities had lost their independence and their fleets, the local authorities could not always employ force; but their coöperation with the Athenian naval forces must have been extremely valuable. The service of the Athenian imperial fleet in keeping down piracy is manifested by the fact that as soon as the empire was overthrown piracy again became rampant.

The great commercial centers in the fifth century were Athens, Ægina, and Corinth. The trade of Corinth in the Ægean was not significant; her interests were mainly in the west, though her favorable situation gave her access by sea to both the east and the west. But the troubles with Corcyra in 433 B.C. hampered her trade with western Hellas and Magna Graecia. Ægina proved a formidable commercial rival of Athens. But in 459-8 she was reduced to the position of a subject state and had to submit to the imperial commercial regulations framed by Athens. At the beginning of the Peloponnesian war, the inhabitants of Ægina were supplanted by Athenian settlers, and the "eyesore of the Piraeus" disappeared.

Athens was not satisfied with making trade and commerce with herself convenient and safe. She did not scruple to use her superior naval power to serve her commercial and economic needs. "Of the continental cities ruled by Athens," says Pseudo-Xenophon,[16] "the larger are held in subjection by their fears, and the smaller by their needs. For no city can escape the necessity of exporting or importing something. This they cannot do unless they become dependent on the rulers of the sea." Isocrates,[17] the orator and publicist, speaking of the first Athenian empire, remarks that "no individual city is self-sufficient in the matter of its products. In some there is a shortage or entire lack; in others there is a surplus. Athens rendered a great service to Greece by providing at the Piraeus a commodious and convenient harbor and mart." He is writing after the downfall of the empire and the inauguration of a more considerate commercial policy in the fourth century, and so prefers to emphasize the commendable aspects of Athenian imperialism. But elsewhere[18] he presents another aspect. Complaining of the activities of pernicious politicians, he says, "They have the assurance to tell us that we ought to imitate our ancestors and not permit those who are unwilling to pay tribute to sail the seas." The means of suppressing the commerce of a recalcitrant city are indicated by the Megarian decree forbidding the Megarians to "use the ports of the empire and the Athenian market."[19] The effect of this prohibition was literally to close the Ægean sea to the Megarians, for without a single friendly harbor in the islands or mainland, they could not venture far afield; they would be confined to coasting voyages about the Peloponnesus.

Food, and raw materials, especially for ship-building, were vital to imperial Athens.

The Athenians are the only people in the Hellenic and the barbarian world [says Pseudo-Xenophon],[20] who are able to control an abundant supply of raw materials. For if a state is rich in timber for ship-building, where will it find a market for it if not with the masters of the sea? If another abounds in iron or bronze or linen yarn, where will it find a market except with the sea lord? Yet this is the stock from which ships are made in Athens. One city yields timber to her, another iron, a third bronze, a fourth linen yarn, a fifth wax, and so on. Moreover, Athens prevents her rivals from transporting goods to other countries than Athens by the threat of driving them from the sea altogether.

The fate of the Megarians shows that this was no idle threat.

There are indications that Athens regulated the trade of the subordinate cities by measures that correspond roughly to the English navigation laws of the eighteenth century, which were intended to centralize colonial trade in the mother country. Under the second Athenian empire the people of Ceos[21] were forbidden to export their ruddle elsewhere than to Athens. This stringent regulation is perhaps a reversion to the more arbitrary policy of the first empire that followed upon the revolt of Ceos in 364-3. There were privileges as well as restrictions. A decree[22] of the late fifth century granted to the inhabitants of Aphytis in Chalcidice the privilege of exporting their products anywhere. Imports were also regulated. Thus a decree of the year 424 B.C. granted to the people of Methone[23] the right of importing a specified quantity of grain from Byzantium. It would seem that this concession was made when the Methonians were excluded from the markets and harbors of Macedonia, from which their grain supplies normally came. There is a trace of some sort of commercial restrictions in the charter of the colony established at Brea in Thessaly in 446-4 B.C.[24] Special commercial privileges were also granted to individuals. For example, Lycon, an Achaean, was given special permission to trade anywhere in the Athenian empire except the gulf of Corinth, which was blockaded.[25]

Privileges imply restrictions. It is evident that neither Aphytis nor Methone enjoyed entire freedom of trade. There are indications of general trade restrictions applicable to the whole empire. There is a provision in the Methonian decree[26] that no general legislation affecting the allies is to apply to Methone unless it is specifically mentioned. This provision is obviously intended to prevent the withdrawal of the special privilege by any general commercial regulation that might be put into force in the future. It is significant in this connection that in the extant "acts of settlement"[27] by which Athens regulated the affairs of her conquered allies there is no reference to trade. The omission is most readily explained by assuming the existence of laws of general application which regulated the trade of the subordinate cities, presumably by requiring surplus grain and essential raw materials to be marketed at Athens. Exceptions affecting particular communities and products were made as occasion required.

Athens did not fail to consult the commercial interests of her allies and subordinates, as was shown in the case of Methone. Not only was permission given to import grain from the Pontus, but also remission of tribute was granted and an embassy was sent to Macedonia to remonstrate with the king for excluding the Methoneans from the Macedonian markets. Without going to the length of rationing the subordinate cities, the Athenians encouraged them to rely as far as possible upon local food supplies by withholding the right of importing grain from areas easily controlled. By means of the Hellespontine guards stationed at Byzantium, they were able to control the distribution of grain from the Pontus.

No doubt it frequently happened that the Athenian commercial interests coincided with those of their allies, but there are indications that sometimes the regulations were regarded as burdensome. The revolt of Thasos was due to a quarrel about the mines and trading posts on the mainland, of which Thasos enjoyed the profits.[28] After the reduction of the island, the inhabitants gave up both the mines and the trading posts. The details of the quarrel are unknown. But it is not unreasonable to suppose that the Thasians were building up their own trade and manufacture by annexing Thracian trading posts. By detaching them from Thasos, Athens brought them under the general regulations requiring exports to come to Athens. A similar motive may have induced Mytilene to try to annex other towns on the island of Lesbos.[29]

An important factor in commerce was coinage. There were a great many currencies which, because of their various degrees of weight and purity, had only a local circulation. The chief currencies that circulated throughout the Ægean were the Corinthian, the Æginetan, and the Athenian.[30] The coins of Athens, owing to their uniform weight and purity, began to prevail even before the Persian wars. Ægina, after its reduction in 459-8 B.C., ceased issuing coins. Athens made an effort to force the subject states to use her coinage. Whatever purpose Aristophanes may have had in writing the *Birds* and picturing a bird city in the clouds, he, at least on occasion, pictures it as a prospective subject city of Athens. But the founders will have nothing of this. The Athenian commissioner is thrust out with kicks and blows.[31] Among the other pests reminiscent of a state of dependence is a statute seller. One of the statutes he offers for sale is as follows: "The Cloud-cuckooburnians are to use the same weights and measures and the self-same coinage as the Olophyxians." Aristophanes is apparently parodying an imperial decree requiring uniformity of coinage, weights, and measures throughout the empire. In 1895 there was discovered on the island of Siphnos[32] a copy of what was presumably the law that Aristophanes is satirizing. The decree forbids the issuing of local coins and takes elaborate precautions to enforce the use of the coinage of Athens. Whether or not this effort to secure uniformity in coinage in the empire was wholly successful we have no means of knowing. It is certain, however, that the standard Athenian coinage was reliable in weight and purity. And we have Aristophanes for a witness[33] that it enjoyed a high reputation and a wide circulation among both Greeks and barbarians. The possession of a medium of exchange that was accepted everywhere was a great advantage to the building up of Athenian commerce in the eastern Mediterranean. Furthermore, the mines at Laurium furnished plenty of silver either for coinage or for export as bullion. It was only during the occupation of Decelea in the last decade of the Peloponnesian war that the supply of silver from Laurium was cut off. Athens made an heroic effort to meet the situation by melting and coining the temple gold in 406 B.C.[34] This was supplemented by a bronze coinage. It was not until 393 B.C. that the silver coinage was again available. In the meantime the empire had been destroyed by the victorious Peloponnesians.

In commerce it is of the utmost importance that security of investments should be assured and credit secured. Reliable means of settling commercial disputes, and reasonable assurance that collections can be made, are highly desirable. Early in their history the Greeks were fully aware that commerce and trade could not flourish without some guaranty that the person and property of the merchant were safe in foreign cities. The guaranty soon took the form of treaties negotiated between friendly states providing for the settlement of disputes between their respective citizens. So widespread was the practice of negotiating such treaties that a commercial state which refused to do so was suspected of an intention to deal arbitrarily with foreigners seeking redress from its citizens.[35]

Cases tried under the provisions of these treaties came before the courts of the city in which the defendant had his domicile, thus insuring the collection of damages assessed. The means for enforcing the verdict in a treaty case were the same for the stranger as for the citizen. It was the usual practice to determine upon and include in these treaties special rules of procedure and special commercial codes. They would naturally be a compromise between the codes of the contracting states. Where Athens was concerned it would appear that her laws tended to prevail, because investigation shows that the procedure of the subordinate cities approximated that of Athens.[36]

Both before and after the formation of the Delian confederacy Athens negotiated judicial treaties with cities both inside and outside the league. When the league was finally changed into an empire and the judicial independence of the cities was materially restricted, there is plenty of evidence that the judicial treaties were not denounced, even where allied cities seceded and were conquered. Athenian merchants and traders still brought commercial suits against their subject allies in their local courts. A passage in Thucydides emphasizes this policy of the Athenians. On the eve of the Peloponnesian war some Athenians happened to be in Sparta on diplomatic business. While they were there, bitter attacks on Athenian treatment of Athenian subjects were made in a conference of Spartan allies. The Athenians asked permission to defend themselves and one of them was permitted to speak before the Spartan assembly. He begins by saying that the relations between an imperial city and its subjects are determined by expediency and not by justice. This, it may be remarked in passing, is a commonplace in Greek political theory. "Men who indulge their natural ambition for empire deserve credit if they are in any way more careful of justice than they need be."[37] Selecting as an example of Athenian magnanimity their handling of the judicial relations, he pointed out that, instead of obliging their subject allies to come to Athens for all commercial cases, the Athenians, waiving their imperial rights, submitted to reciprocity with their political inferiors, and their merchants enforced contracts by suits in the courts of the subject states. For controversial purposes the speaker has made good use of this aspect of Athenian policy; but it may be doubted if Athenians were making any concession to justice. In the interest of their commerce nothing could be more expedient than to continue to permit treaty cases to come before the courts of a subject city when one of its citizens was being sued by an Athenian. This policy is a mark of Athenian sound commonsense and awareness of material interests in the administration of the empire.

In the processes of litigation the interests and convenience of merchants, both citizen and alien, were carefully consulted. Cases arising out of written commercial contracts were classed as "mercantile suits," which were governed by special rules.[38] Unnecessary or vexatious litigation was discouraged by the imposition of a penalty amounting to one-sixth of the sum claimed, if the litigant failed to obtain one-fifth of the votes. Interference with business was reduced to a minimum by the requirement that these cases could be tried only in the winter months when navigation was suspended. As one or both litigants was often a foreigner, there was danger that the damages awarded might not be paid at all, or at least not promptly. As a safeguard against this eventuality the court was empowered to imprison the loser pending satisfaction of the verdict. These regulations are drawn mainly from speeches attributed to Demosthenes, and are not known to have been in force in the fifth century. But a passage in Aristophanes' *Parliament of Women* (392 B.C.)[39] shows that a merchant enjoyed some privileges in litigation. A young man about whom two old hags quarrel resorts to various expedients to escape their unwelcome attentions. One is a claim that he is a merchant. Van Leeuwen is undoubtedly right in rejecting the view that the poet has in mind exemption from military service. Rather, the young man is asking to have the case postponed until the season for "mercantile suits." In support of this view it may be noted that the other devices for escape suggested by the young man are all legal.

Demosthenes,[40] when defending a money-lender, takes occasion to urge upon the jury the advisability of upholding the sanctity of contracts in the interest of Athenian trade, and Isocrates[41] laments the tendency to regard equity rather than law. "Strict adherence to the letter of the law is more to the interest of the borrower than the present-day tendency to look to the equity of a particular case rather than the law," because it encourages the capitalists to lend their money more freely. Democratic juries may well have been inclined to favor the poor man when hard pressed by a money-lender, but as between the capitalist and the merchant, who often were resident aliens or foreigners, there was little to choose.

In the interest of trade the Piraeus was fortified so as to protect the merchants who resorted there from hostile raids in war time. An incident in the fourth century shows what havoc could be wrought by a sea raid on the Piraeus.[42] The Spartan commander stationed in Ægina conceived the idea of a raid on the commerce in the Piraeus. The Athenians, confident in their sea power, failed to take proper protective measures. The Spartans slipped in and towed off a number of laden merchant ships, captured the crews of others as prisoners, and even going ashore seized merchants and owners engaged in business in the mart. As the enemy coasted along on their way back to Ægina they picked up fishing craft and ferry boats from the islands as well as merchantmen laden with grain or merchandise.

A special mercantile port was laid out in the time of Themistocles with adequate docks and warehouses. There were also colonnaded buildings for the display of the merchants' wares. These were built by Pericles.[43] Foreigners were encouraged "by equality of intercourse between aliens and citizens" to settle in the city and the port because "they were needed on account of the multitude of handicrafts and the fleet."[44] As the empire grew in wealth, power, and culture, it was inevitable that large numbers, both of subjects and strangers, should find it advantageous or necessary to resort to the city which was at once the administrative center of a great empire and the "school of all Hellas." And every increase in the number of those who sojourned or settled in the city brought a corresponding increase in the imports and exports.

The Athenian system of settling citizens in the territory of the subject states, either as a result of agreement or of conquest, had some bearing on the expansion of Athenian commerce. These settlers were known as *cleruchs* (holders of lots, κληροῦχοι), because, when too many applied for land, the lot was used. In a period of fifty years as many as ten thousand cleruchs were sent out to various parts of the empire.[45] As these settlers retained Athenian citizenship and had the right to hold real property, it was only natural to expect that they would make use of their home associations and thus increase the business of the Piraeus.

Trading companies are known to have been organized in the fifth century, but we have no information regarding their operations. Judged by modern standards, the banking system was crude. Clearing houses were unknown. But merchants could avoid the risk of transporting money from one city to another. For example, an alien client of Isocrates,[46] resident in Athens, had money owing to him in Pontus. A fellow-countryman, on departing for home, advanced the amount to the creditor in Athens and collected the debt in Pontus. No doubt, between large trading centers this could often be done with advantage to both parties.

The imperial restrictions upon the judicial autonomy of the subject states had a very practical purpose in view.

And the Athenian people seem to take a wrong course in this also, that they force the allies to sail to Athens for the settlement of law suits; however, they reckon up all the advantages that are in this to their party (i.e., the democracy). First of all they draw pay (as dicasts) from the court fees. Next, while sitting at home, without dispatching ships, they have the cities of the allies under their control, and they uphold in the courts the friends of democracy, and bring destruction upon those opposed to it, whereas if the several communities had justice administered in their own cities, in their hostility to Athens they would bring destruction, death, banishment, and loss of civil rights upon those of their countrymen who were attached to the popular party at Athens.[47]

The restrictions of the judicial power of the subordinate cities are nowhere set forth in detail. From the statement "they force the allies to sail to Athens for the settlement of law suits," one might suppose that the local courts were abolished. But this was not the fact. There is plenty of evidence that local courts continued to function even in cities that had revolted and been reduced.[48] In 446 B.C. the revolt of Euboea was crushed. The decree modifying the agreement of the surrender of Chalcis has been partially preserved. In it provision is made for referring to Athens all cases involving the penalties of banishment, death, and loss of civil and political rights. These cases were not appeals, but reserved cases.[49]

An *obiter dictum* of a client of Antiphon[50] to the effect that no city in the empire could inflict the death penalty without the confirmation of the Athenian people, has been used to prove that there was a general law applicable to all subject cities depriving them of the right to inflict the death penalty. This view is confirmed by a statement in Pseudo-Xenophon's *Constitution of Athens*.[51] The Athenian democracy, it is asserted, feared the upper classes in the subordinate cities, and adopted measures to suppress them as political factors.

With regard to the allies, the popular party [in Athens] has a hatred for, and brings, as appears, malicious accusations against, the best men among the allies, knowing that if the rich and responsible classes in the cities become strong, the ascendancy of the democratic party in Athens will endure but for a very short time; for this reason, then, they deprive the good of their civic rights and property, and get them exiled, and put them to death.

It is evident that the Athenians reserved for their courts the right to inflict the penalties of death, banishment, and *atimia* (loss of civic rights). This was not such a reprehensible and high-handed policy as at first it seems. The Athenians, familiar with the Greek custom of using the courts to ruin political enemies, took measures to nullify such efforts by depriving the local courts of the power to inflict serious penalties on friends of Athens. Bearing in mind the anti-democratic attitude of the writer of this essay, we need not be misled into believing that in the courts the good were always condemned and the bad acquitted. From the Athenian standpoint the system worked two ways. It prevented the enemies of imperialism in the subordinate cities from embarrassing and thwarting the friends of Athens. At the same time, it put into the hands of Athens a most effective means for dealing with the anti-imperialists in the subject cities, and for keeping a firm hold on the empire by trying them in Athens. A sentence of banishment by an Athenian court included the whole empire.[52]

The subject cities were permitted to lodge an appeal against the quadrennial assessment of tribute before Athenian judicial officials known as "introducers" in Athens.[53] These were classed as "monthly suits." The Athenian courts were notoriously congested in the fifth century. In order to provide for matters that did not brook delay, they arranged that they must be brought to trial within a month of filing suit. It is obvious that it was to the interest of Athenians to have questions affecting their finances settled speedily. The subject states were prevented from interposing delays indefinitely.

Provision was also made for prosecuting in Athenian courts individuals suspected of inciting a city not to pay its tribute or in any way interfering with the carrying out of the provisions of the laws governing the collection and payment of tribute. These also were "monthly suits," and were lodged before the "overseers," who were imperial officers appointed to deal with all matters affecting the collecting of the tribute. The decree from which this information is drawn is conjecturally dated 424-423 B.C.

Cases of treason in the empire would naturally be tried in Athens. Aristophanes refers to this type of case in the *Wasps*,[54] where a native of one of the Thrace-ward cities is to be tried for conspiring with the Spartans under Brasidas to betray his native city. It is evidently a common kind of charge to bring in the Athenian courts; else it would not have served the purpose of Aristophanes.

Much has been said in favor of Athenian imperialism in the way of apology, and much more has been said against it by both ancient and modern writers.[55] The Athenians themselves took little or no pains to justify the system. Pericles[56] did say that Athens was the "school of Hellas," and claimed that Athens was a mistress whom no subjects need be ashamed to serve. But in the last analysis the Athenians were ready to admit that from their standpoint imperialism was exploitation in the interest of the rulers. Doubtless there were many by-products of imperialism that were beneficial to the subject communities. This phase of the question has been pretty thoroughly explored. But there is one service of Athenian imperialism that has not been adequately emphasized. Democracy seems to have suited the Greek political temper better than any other form of government. And for three-quarters of a century Athens "kept the Ægean safe for democracy."[57] In turn the local democracies, knowing that their continued existence depended upon Athens, accepted imperialism with as good grace as was to be expected from Greeks, who were always self-determinists at heart.

NOTES

(1) i. 1 ff.; iii. 10. tr. by Brooks. Sometimes he is cited as the Old Oligarch. The work belongs to the early years of the Peloponnesian war (428-424 B.C.).

(2) Cf. Wade-Gery, *Classical Quarterly*, XXV, 1 ff.

(3) Aristotle *Ath. Pol.* iii. 6.

(4) *Solon* xiv.

(5) Bonner and Smith, *Administration of Justice from Homer to Aristotle*, pp. 154 ff.

(6) *Ath. Pol.* xiv.

(7) *Ibid.* xvi. 2.

(8) Thuc. vi. 54.

(9) Aristotle *Ath.Pol.*xx-xxi;Herod. v. 66, 69-73.

(10) For the development of the judiciary, which constituted such an important element in popular sovereignty in Athens, see *infra*, pp. 25 ff.

(11) *Solon* xix.

(12) Bonner and Smith, *op. cit.*, pp. 200 ff.; pp. 335 ff.

(13) *Ibid.*, pp. 200 ff.

(14) There is some uncertainty as to what extent, if any, the lot was used before the time of Cleisthenes. Cf. Aristotle *Ath. Pol.* viii. 1; xxii. 5. Ferguson, *Klio*, IV, 1 ff.; Smith, *Trans. Am. Phil. Assoc.* LVI, 113, *n.* 38.

(15) Aristotle *Ath. Pol.* xxii. 2.

(16) For the date see Bonner and Smith, *op. cit.*, p. 195. For the quorum theory see Bonner,"The Minimum Vote in Ostracism," *Class. Phil.* VIII, 223-225. Busolt - Swoboda, *Staatskunde*, p. 885, *n.* 2.

(17) Aristotle *Ath. Pol.* xvi. 10 cites an old law to the effect that anyone who attempted to set up a tyranny should be disfranchised.

(18) *Ath. Pol.* xxiii. 1.

(19) *Ath. Pol.* viii. 4.

(20) *Ath. Pol.* xxv. 2. Cf. Wilamowitz, *Aristoteles und Athen*, ii, 93 ff.

(21) Smith, *TAPA*, LVI (1925), 114, *n.* 39.

(22) Verrall,*Eumenides of Aeschylus*, XLIX; Sidgwick, *Aeschylus, Eumenides*, p. 25; Bury, *History of Greece*, p. 348.

(23) *Areopagiticus.*

(24) Aristotle *Ath. Pol.* xxvi. 2.

(25) *Ibid.* vii. 4. Cf. Gilbert, *The Constitutional Antiquities of Sparta and Athens*, p. 157, *n.* 1.

(26) Thuc. viii. 65. 3; Aristotle, *op. cit.*, xxix. 5.

(27) Lysias xxxiv.

(28) Cf. *Cambridge Ancient History (C.A.H.)* V, pp. 103-104.

(29) Headlam, *Election by Lot*, pp. 19 ff.

(30) Gilbert, *op. cit.*, p. 218, *n.* 3.

(31) *Ibid.*, 217, *n.* 2.

(32) 32 B.

(33) Xenophon *Memorabilia* i. 2. 9.

(34) Lipsius, *Das Attische Recht*, pp. 269 ff.

(35) *Knights* 447. Lipsius, *op. cit.*, p. 275.

(36) xvi. 9.

(37) lix. 72-78.

(38) Aristotle *Ath. Pol.* xliii. 4.

(39) xii. xx.

(40) vi. 43.

(41) Xen. *Memor.* i. 2. 9.
(42) Aristotle, *op. cit.*, xliii. ff. for the organization of the council.
(43) *Ath. Pol.* iii. 2.
(44) Aristotle *Ath. Pol.* xliii. 4-6.
(45) Cf. Bonner and Smith, *op. cit.*, pp. 204 ff. for the quorum.
(46) Lysias xxxi. 33.
(47) xxii. 2. Cf. Bonner and Smith, *op. cit.*, pp. 338 ff.
(48) *Ath. Pol.* i. 3.
(49) *Ath. Pol.* xxvi.

(50) Gertrude Smith, "Athenian Casualty Lists," *Class. Phil.*, XIV, 351 ff.
(51) 609 ff.
(52) *Eux.* 7-8.
(53) vii. 23.
(54) i. 2.
(55) *Politics* iv. 9. Cf. vi. 1. 15.
(56) ii. 40, Jowett's trans.
(57) Plutarch *Solon* v.
(58) *Ath. Pol.* xli. 2.

(1) xviii. 497 ff.
(2) Bonner and Smith, *op. cit.*, pp. 32 ff.
(3) *Politics* 1285 B.
(4) *Theogony* 81 ff.
(5) Cf. Hesiod *Works and Days* 27 ff.
(6) *Ibid.* p. 228.
(7) *Od.* ii. 28-29.
(8) *Od.* xxiv. 439 ff.
(9) Lipsius, *op. cit.*, p. 6; Glotz, *La Cité*, p. 66.
(10) Bonner and Smith, *op. cit.*, pp. 22-23.
(11) Aelian *Varia Historia* iii. 38.
(12) Busolt-Swoboda, *Staatskunde*, II, 786.
(13) Aristotle *Ath. Pol.* lvi. 2.
(14) Bonner and Smith, *op. cit.*, pp. 88 ff.
(15) 431 ff., Way's translation.
(16) *C.I.A.* I, 61. This inscription is reproduced with a commentary and translation by Bonner and Smith, *op. cit.*, pp. 112 ff.
(17) Aristotle *Ath. Pol.* iii. 5.
(18) Smith, *TAPA*, LVI, 106. Cf. Bonner and Smith, *op. cit.*, pp. 151-162.
(19) Aristotle *Ath. Pol.* ix. 1.
(20) Calhoun, *Growth of Criminal Law*, p. 75.
(21) Aristotle *Ath. Pol.* viii. 4.
(22) *Ibid.*
(23) Bonner and Smith, *op. cit.*, pp. 197 ff.
(24) Lipsius, *op. cit.*, p. 32. Cf. Busolt-Swoboda, *op. cit.*, p. 883.
(25) Cf. *supra*, p. 7.
(26) Pseudo-Xen. *Ath. Pol.* i. 18.
(27) Cf. Schol. *ad Eur. Orestes*, 1648.
(28) *Ath. Pol.* xxv. 3.

(29) Bonner and Smith, *op. cit.*, pp. 270 ff.
(30) Cf. Lipsius, *op. cit.*, pp. 36 and 384.
(31) Lipsius, *op. cit.*, p. 360; *C.A.H.* V, 382.
(32) 590-591.
(33) *Eux.* 1. ff.
(34) For the arguments in favor of this view see Bonner and Smith, *op. cit.*, pp. 296 ff.
(35) Plut. *Pericles* ix; Aristotle *Ath. Pol.* xxvii. 3. Cf. Bonner and Smith, *op. cit.*, pp. 226 ff.
(36) Aristotle *Ath. Pol.* xxiv.
(37) *Ibid.* xxvii. 4. Cf. Busolt-Swoboda, *op. cit.*, p. 897.
(38) Lipsius, *op. cit.*, p. 136.
(39) For arguments against the accepted view that fifth-century panels contained 501 dicasts, see Bonner and Smith, *op. cit.*, pp. 235 ff.
(40) Pseudo-Xen. *op. cit.* iii. 7. Cf. Lipsius, *op. cit.*, pp. 139 ff. Hommel, *Heliaea*, pp. 115 ff.
(41) See Hommel, *op. cit.*, pp. 11 ff., for a full discussion of the system described by Aristotle *Ath. Pol.* lxiii ff.
(42) *In Leocratem* 6.
(43) i. 2.
(44) 39-41.
(45) iii. 6.
(46) i. 73 ff.
(47) Aristotle *Ath. Pol.* lv. 2.
(48) Lipsius, *op. cit.*, pp. 286 ff.
(49) Gilbert, *op. cit.*, pp. 299 ff.
(50) Aristotle *Ath. Pol.* vii.
(51) Demos. xxiv. 139; Polyb. xii. 6.; Stobaeus 44, 21.

(52) Lipsius, *op. cit.*, pp. 383 ff.
(53) *Politics* 1292 A.
(54) Aeschines *In Ctesiphontem* 194.
(55) Goligher, *Hermathena* XIV, 481-515. Cf. Calhoun, *Growth of Criminal Law*, p. 55.
(56) Lipsius, *op. cit.*, p. 969 ff.
(57) *Infra*, pp. 174 ff.
(58) Robertson, "Administration of Justice in the Athenian Empire," *Univ. of Toronto Studies, History and Economics*, IV, pp. 48 ff.
(59) 767C. Cf. Theoretical Constitution of Hippodamus: Aristotle *Politics* 1267 B.

FOOTNOTES TO CHAPTER III

(1) Thuc. ii. 40.
(2) Aristotle *Ath. Pol.* xxiv. 3. Cf. *C.A.H.* V, 104-6.
(3) 515 E.
(4) Xen. *Memor.* iii. 7. 6.
(5) *Protagoras* 319 D.
(6) Cf. Hicks and Hill, *Greek Historical Inscriptions*, p. 41.
(7) *Eux.* 30.
(8) xxi. 189.
(9) xxiii. 4.
(10) v. 12.
(11) *Politics* 1313 B. But Aristotle himself used it of men he esteemed, e.g. *Pol.* 1305 A.
(12) *Memor.* iii. 6 ff.
(13) Plato *Protagoras* 318 E.
(14) Foucart, *Bull. de Corr. Hell.* IV (1880), pp. 225 ff. Cf. F. D. Smith, *Athenian Political Commissions*, pp. 17 ff.
(15) II. 67.
(16) *Ath. Pol.* xxviii, 1.
(17) 191-193.
(18) *Knights* 1115 ff.
(19) II. 65. 9.
(20) *Politics* 1305 A.
(21) Aristotle *Ath. Pol.* xxiii. 3.
(22) Plut. *Pericles* xxiii.
(23) 128 ff. The leaders were Eucrates, Lysicles, and Cleon.
(24) Aristophanes *Acharn.* 378 ff.; Aristotle *Ath. Pol.* xxviii. 3.
(25) Aristophanes *Clouds* 876.
(26) Andocides i. 133.
(27) Plato *Ion* 541 D.
(28) *C.A.H.* V, 344.
(29) Sundwall, "Epigraphische Beiträge zur Social-Politischen Geschichte Athens," *Klio*, Ergänzungsband, 1903-1906, Beiheft IV. Cf. Plato *Republic* VIII. 565 A.
(30) *C.A.H.* V, 344; Bury, *History of Greece*, p. 498.
(31) Aristotle, *Ath. Pol.* xli.
(32) Plut. *Nicias* xi. Cf. *supra*, p. 7, for the establishment of ostracism.
(33) *C.A.H.* V, 218.
(34) Lofberg, *Sycophancy in Athens*, pp. 26 ff.
(35) *Ibid.*, pp. 51-52.
(36) Antiphon vi.
(37) Grote VI, 246. Cf. Calhoun, *Athenian Clubs in Politics and Litigation.*
(38) Calhoun, *Growth of Criminal Law*, p. 119.
(39) *Hermathena* IV, 86.
(40) Antiphon *Frag.* 12; Andocides i. 17.
(41) viii. 67.
(42) Cf. *supra*, pp. 5-6. Bonner, *Lawyers and Litigants in Ancient Athens*, p. 6; Calhoun, *Growth of Criminal Law*, pp. 105-107.
(43) *C.A.H.* V, 477 ff., for a discussion of the various trials.
(44) Demos. *De Corona* 249.

FOOTNOTES TO CHAPTER IV

(1) Eurip. *Phoen.* 392.
(2) Eurip. *Ion* 671-672.
(3) Plato *Rep.* 557B; *Gorgias* 461E.
(4) Pseudo-Xen. i. 2 and 6.
(5) Plut. *Solon* xxi.
(6) 934 E.
(7) Hitzig, *Injuria*, 25.
(8) x. 6 ff.
(9) Demos. xxi. 35.
(10) *Ibid.* 57. 30.
(11) Aristotle *Ath. Pol.* liii.
(12) Demos. *De Corona*, 5.
(13) x.
(14) Hitzig, *op. cit.*, p. 26; Thonissen, *Le Droit Pénal Ath.*, p. 280; Lipsius, *op. cit.*, pp. 648 ff.
(15) Cf. Forsyth, *Hortensius, or The Advocate*, p. 51; Bredif, *Demosthenes*, Chap. VIII.
(16) Aeschines *In Ctesiphontem* 2.
(17) *Acharn.* 45.
(18) Anaximenes 18; Isocrates vi.1-6.
(19) Plut. *Moralia* 804 B.
(20) *Memor.* iii. 6. 1. ff.
(21) Demos. 5.
(22) Isoc. vii. 58.
(23) viii. 14.
(24) *Apol.* 31 E. Cf. Plato *Protagoras* 319.
(25) Thuc. ii. 65. 7; vi. 89.
(26) Herod. vi. 136; Plato *Gorgias* 516 E.
(27) xx. 100.
(28) Cf. Bonner and Smith, *op. cit.*, pp. 208-209.
(29) Aristotle *Ath. Pol.* 43, 5.
(30) The favorable attitude of the public was evidenced by the readiness of many to go bail for the accused.
(31) Xenophon *Hell.* i. 7. 35.
(32) ii. 43.
(33) Aristotle *Ath. Pol.* xliii. 5.
(34) Bury, *op. cit.*, p. 565.
(35) Hyper. iv. 29.
(36) Hager, *Jour. Phil.* IV, 89, for a full citation of cases.
(37) *Supra*, p. 63.
(38) The *locus classicus* on *atimia* is Andocides i. 73 ff. Cf. *infra*, pp. 86-87.
(39) Lipsius, *op. cit.*, p. 280; Kock, "Dokimasia," *in* Pauly-Wissowa-Kroll.
(40) Aeschines *Hypothesis* i.
(41) x. 1 and 22.
(42) Lysias x. 12 and 24.
(43) I. 32. Thalheim (Teubner) and Gernet (Budé), in their editions of Lysias, regard the case as a *dokimasia*.
(44) iii. 43, 4 ff.
(45) viii. 1.
(46) *C.A.H.* V, 109.

FOOTNOTES TO CHAPTER V

(1) 73 ff.
(2) Aristotle *Ath. Pol.* xxvi. 4.
(3) Gilbert, *op. cit.*, p. 184.
(4) Plato *Crito*, 50 D.
(5) Plut. *Solon* xxii.
(6) Aristotle *Ath. Pol.* xlii.
(7) Forbes, *Greek Physical Education*, pp. 109 ff., with a complete bibliography.
(8) *Peace* 44.
(9) Xenophon *Memorabilia* iii.12.5.
(10) Thuc. ii. 39.
(11) Thuc. i. 105. 4. Cf. ii. 13. 7.
(12) Taylor, "The Athenian Ephebic Oath," *Class. Jour.* XIII, 495 ff. The oath is not mentioned by Aristotle, doubtless because it was not a novelty.
(13) Plut. *Alcib.* xv. 4. Forbes, *op. cit.*, p. 123.
(14) Aristotle *Ath. Pol.* viii. 5.
(15) *Ibid.* xiv. 2.
(16) Plut. *Solon* xviii.
(17) *Ath. Pol.* i. 3.
(18) Thuc. ii. 37.
(19) Cf. Thuc. iii. 82-83 for the horrors of civil strife in Greece during war times.
(20) Pseudo-Xen. iii. 12-13.

(21) Thuc. ii. 60.
(22) Grundy, *Thuc. and the Hist. of His Age*, p. 80.
(23) Grundy, *op. cit.*, pp. 104 ff.
(24) *C.I.A.* I. 432-62. Cf. Gertrude Smith, "Athenian Casualty Lists," *Class. Phil.* XIV, 351 ff.
(25) Aristotle *Ath. Pol.* xxvii. 3.
(26) Lysias xvi. 17; Demos. xxv. 76.
(27) *Ath. Pol.* xxiv. 3.
(28) Aristotle *Ath. Pol.* xli. 3; Aristophanes *Acharnians* 19-20.
(29) Cf. Lofberg, *Sycophancy in Athens*, pp. 26 ff.
(30) Cf. Bonner, *Lawyers and Litigants*, p. 47.
(31) *Knights* 573-576.
(32) Plato *Apol.* 36 D.
(33) *C.A.H.* V, 344.
(34) Aristotle *Ath. Pol.* xlix, 4 ; cf. Lysias xxiv.
(35) Thuc. ii. 40.
(36) Plato *Apol.* 31 C.
(37) 730 D.
(38) Thuc. ii. 43.
(39) Thuc. ii. 36. 4; ii. 38; ii. 41.
(40) (Demos.) 47.
(41) Grundy, *op. cit.*, p. 89, *n.* 2.

(1) *Modern Democracies*, p. 520.

(2) Plut. *Solon* viii.

(3) Cf. *supra*, p. 1.

(4) Aristotle *Rhetoric* i. 7. 34.

(5) Thucydides ii. 44–45. Cf. Simonides in Plutarch *Moralia* 786 B.

(6) Aristotle *Rhetoric* iii. 10. 7.

(7) Eupolis *Frag.* 94.

(8) Thuc. viii. 68.

(9) Diodorus Siculus xii. 53.

(10) The text is that of Sauppe. *Oratores Attici* ii. 130.

(11) iii. 38. Trans. by Jowett.

(12) Deliberative or parliamentary, and epideictic or display oratory.

(13) Jebb, *Attic Orators*, ii, 373.

(14) Herodotus iii. 80 ff.

(15) i. 22.

(16) Jebb, *op. cit.*, ii. 431.

(17) *History of Greece*, IX, 167 and 217.

(18) Plut. *Solon* xxix.

(19) Cf. Scott, *The Unity of Homer*.

(20) Flickinger, *The Greek Theater and Its Drama*, pp. 21–24.

(21) Each poet offered a tragic trilogy and a satyr-play.

(22) *Fragmenta* 256 K; cf. *Frag.* 15 K, and Chionides *Frag.* 4 K.

(23) *Peace* 803–804.

(24) Tyrants with literary aspirations are said to have punished their critics. Cf. Pseudo-Plutarch *Life of Antiphon* 14; Diodorus Siculus xv. 6.

(25) Haigh, *The Attic Theater*, p. 48.

(26) For instances of popular disapproval, see Aristophanes *Knights* 524–525; Aristotle *Politics* 17. 1 B. Pleas for popular favor are found in Aristophanes *Knights* 37 ff.; *Clouds* 518 ff.

(27) Aristophanes *Wasps* 220.

(28) Cf. *supra*, p. 9.

(29) Cf. Flickinger, *op. cit.*, pp. 183 ff., for the importance of actors.

(30) *Rhetoric* iii. 16.

(31) Haigh, *Tragic Drama of the Greeks*, p. 404.

(32) Pseudo-Plutarch *Life of Lycurgus* 841 F.

(33) Aristotle *Poetics* iv. 12.

(34) Flickinger, *op. cit.*, pp. 35 ff.

(35) Capps, *Greek Comedy*, in *Greek Literature*, p. 135. (A series of lectures delivered at Columbia University, 1912.)

(36) ii. 18.

(37) Cf. Starkie's *Excursus* in his edition of the *Acharnians*; Capps, *Am. Jour. Philol.*, XXVIII, 190 ff.

(38) Cf. Max Radin, *Freedom of Speech in Ancient Athens, A.J. P.* XLVIII (1927), 215 ff., for a complete discussion of the subject and an attractive suggestion regarding the date of the law dealing with "actionable words."

(39) The punitive power of the council was limited to a fine of 500 drachmas. Cf. Bonner and Smith, *op. cit.*, pp. 337 ff.

(40) Lines 501 ff.

(41) Lines 515 ff.
(42) Capps, *The Introduction of Comedy into the City Dionysia*, Decennial Publications (Univ. Chicago, 1903).
(43) Capps, *Comedy*, p. 133.
(44) *Ibid.*, p. 134.
(45) *Nicias* xxix.
(46) Lines 738 ff.
(47) *Clouds* 539.
(48) Cornford, *The Origin of Attic Comedy*, pp. 116-117.

(49) *Der Dialog*, pp. 49-50.
(50) *Ibid.*, pp. 53 ff.
(51) Butcher, *Greek Genius*, p. 190.
(52) G. L. Dickinson, *Plato and His Dialogues*, p. 56.
(53) Pike, *Roman Epistolography*, p. 97.
(54) Cf. Victor, *De Epistolis; Ars Rhetorica.*
(55) Aristotle *Politics* iii. 11. 2.

(1) Aristotle *Politics* 1285 B; Homer *Iliad* iii. 245 ff.; 275 ff.

(2) Nilsson, *Greek Religion*, p. 243.

(3) Plut. *Theseus* 25.

(4) Nilsson, *op. cit.*, pp. 191, 244.

(5) *Politics* 1319 B.

(6) Gilbert, *The Constitutional Antiquities of Sparta and Athens*, p. 192.

(7) Suidas, *s.v.* φράτορες.

(8) Isaeus iii. 76.

(9) Isaeus vi. 64.

(10) Aristotle *Ath. Pol.* 43. 6.

(11) Pseudo-Xenophon *Ath. Pol.* iii. 2 and 8.

(12) *Alcibiades* ii. 148 E.

(13) Thuc. ii. 38.

(14) *Laws* 653 D. Bury trans.

(15) *Op. cit.* ii. 9.

(16) Kalinka, *Die Pseudoxenophontische* ΑΘΗΝΑΙΩΝ ΠΟΛΙΤΕΙΑ, p. 278; *C.A.H.* V, 279.

(17) vii. 81.

(18) Nilsson, *op. cit.*, pp. 26 ff.

(19) Pausanias viii. 2. 1.

(20) Mommsen, *Feste der Stadt Athen*, p. 61.

(21) Aristophanes *Lysistrata* 641.

(22) Aristotle *Ath. Pol.* lx.

(23) Homer *Iliad* vi. 269 ff.

(24) This was especially true of the festivals in honor of Dionysus, discussed *supra*, p. 118.

(25) Cf. *infra*, p. 159.

(26) Xenophon *Hell.* i. 4. 20. Cf. Grote, VII, 391 ff.

(27) Mommsen, *op. cit.*, p. 430.

(28) Line 122.

(29) 118 A.

(30) In a recent publication of the Committee on the Costs of Medical Care entitled *The Healing Cults*, it is estimated that their votaries expend $125,-000,000 annually for "treatments."

(31) viii. 6. 15.

(32) Trans. by Rogers. Pp. xx ff. of his edition of Aristophanes' *Plutus*.

(33) Plato *Phaedo* 117 B.

(34) Thuc. i. 96.

(35) Xenophon *Memor.* iii. 8. 10.

(36) Antiphon vi. 39.

(37) Demosthenes xxxvi. 15.

(38) viii. 15 ff.

(39) Thuc. ii. 21.

(40) Thuc. viii. 1.

(41) *Knights* 61 ff.

(42) *Knights* 1013; *Birds* 978.

(43) In defense of his war policy Cleon says that Athens will rule over all Hellas, for the oracles say that some day Demos shall sit in judgment at five obols per day (*Knights* 798 ff.). This is a convenient reminder that Cleon had raised the dicasts' pay to three obols.

(44) *Birds* 716 ff.

(45) Antiphon v. 82-83; Andocides i. 137.

(46) Plut. *Solon* xix; Andocides i. 78. Cf. Bonner and Smith, *op. cit.*, 104 ff.

(47) Plut. *Solon* xii; Thuc. i. 126.

(48) Thuc. i. 128.
(49) *C.A.H.* V, 286 ff. Andocides i and ii; Thuc. vi. 27-29; 53.
(50) Cf. *supra*, p. 141.
(51) *Lysistrata* 1093-1094.
(52) Cf. Plut. *Pericles* xxxii.
(53) Plut. *Pericles* xxxii.

(54) Plut. *Nicias* xxiii. 3. Cf. Schol. on Aristophanes *Knights* 1088.
(55) Line 830.
(56) *Papyri Oxyrhynchus* ix. 153.
(57) Aelian, *Varia Historia*, ii. 13.
(58) Diog. Laert. ii. 40.
(59) *C.A.H.*, V. 390 ff.

(1) Thuc. iii. 104.
(2) These Athenian officials were probably not instituted until 454, when the treasury was moved to Athens. *C.A.H.* V, 46.
(3) I. 99.
(4) Wilamowitz, *Von des Attischen Reichs Beherrlichkeit. Eine Festrede*, p. 11.
(5) Foucart, *Bull. corr. hell.*, IV (1880), 225 ff.
(6) Gilbert, *op. cit.*, p. 426.
(6) *Pericles*, xvii. Cf. *C.A.H.* V, 93.
(7) Plut. *Pericles* xii.
(8) Aristotle *Ath. Pol.* xxiv.
(9) Pseudo-Xenophon i. 17-18.
(10) i. 6. Dakyn's trans.
(11) Pseudo-Xen. *Ath. Pol.* ii. 7.
(12) Thuc. ii. 38. Smith's trans.
(13) i. 13.
(14) Plut. *Cimon* viii.
(15) Demos. 58. 53 ff.
(16) *Ath. Pol.* ii. 3.
(17) *Panegyricus* 42.
(18) *Peace* 36.
(19) Thuc. i. 139: Aristophanes *Acharnians* 533-534.
(20) *Ath. Pol.* ii. 11, 12.
(21) *C.I.A.* ii. 546. Hicks and Hill, *op. cit.*, no. 137.
(22) *I.G.* I. 41.
(23) *I.G.* I. 40. Hicks and Hill, *op. cit.*, no. 60.
(24) *I.G.* I. 31. Hicks and Hill, *op. cit.*, no. 41.
(25) Dittenberger, *Sylloge²*, 46.
(26) Hicks and Hill, *op. cit.*, no. 60, 42-48.

(27) These documents are conveniently assembled in Hill, *Sources for Greek History*, Chap. I, 125-130. Cf. p. 195. They are all found also in Hicks and Hill, *op. cit.*, with bibliographies and notes.
(28) Thuc. i. 100.
(29) Thuc. iii. 2.
(30) *C.A.H.* V, 23.
(31) Aristophanes *Birds* 1020 ff.
(32) *I.G.* xii. 5. 480.
(33) *Frogs* 725 ff.
(34) Head, *Historia Numorum*, p. 373.
(35) Thuc. I. 37. 3.
(36) Weber, *Att. Processrecht in d. Att. Seebundstaaten.*
(37) Cf. Bonner, *Class. Phil.* XIV, 284 ff.
(38) Lipsius, *op. cit.*, pp. 631 ff.; 852, 901 ff.
(39) 1027. Cf. Van Leeuwen's note on Aristophanes, *Plutus*, 904.
(40) Demos. 56. 48.
(41) *Areopagiticus* 33.
(42) Xenophon *Hell.* v. 1. 18 ff.
(43) *C.A.H.* V, 18.
(44) Pseudo-Xenophon *Ath. Pol.* i. 12.
(45) Gilbert, *op. cit.*, p. 447.
(46) xvii, 35.
(47) Pseudo-Xenophon *Ath. Pol.* i. 16 ff.
(48) Thuc. iv. 130.
(49) Hicks and Hill, *op. cit.*, no. 40. Cf. Bonner and Smith, *op. cit.*, p. 314, *n.* 2.
(50) v. 47.

(51) i. 14 and 16. Cf. Robertson, *Administration of Justice in the Athenian Empire*, pp. 43 ff. There is some difficulty in the reading; but whether we read ὃι πλέονες (the popular party) or ὃι ἐκπλέοντες ("Athenians going overseas"), the result is the same.

(52) Hicks and Hill, *op. cit.*, no. 32; Xen. *Hell.* i. 5. 19.

(53) Robertson, *op. cit.*, pp. 48 ff.

(54) *Wasps* 287-289.

(55) Cf. *C.A.H.* V, 94 ff.; 111-112; Robertson, *op. cit.*, pp. 72 ff.

(56) Thuc. ii. 41.

(57) The view that Athens imposed democracy on her subjects (*C.A.H.* V, 471 ff.) is scarcely supported by the evidence. Cf. Robertson, "Oligarchy and Democracy in the Athenian Empire," *Class. Phil.*, XXVIII, 50 ff.

INDEX

INDEX

Achilles, shield of, 25
Acts of settlement, 166
ἀδικία, 77
Administration of justice: under Solon, 3; in assembly and heliastic courts, 22, 35; Greek regard for, 25; in Heroic Age, 25; under aristocracy, 26
Aeschines: impeachment of, 21; prosecution of Timarchus by, 35, 82
Aeschylus: *Eumenides*, 9, 121; *Persians*, 109, 121
Agora in Heroic Age, 2, 27
Agyrrhius, 56, 57
ἄκριτοι, 19
Alcibiades: attempted ostracism of, 58; in assembly, 76; profanation of Mysteries by, 141, 152
Alcmaeonidae: expulsion of Pisistratidae by, 4, 151; *see also* Cleisthenes
Aliens, 87
Amnesty of 403 B.C., 92
Anacharsis, 23
Anaxagoras, impeachment of, 65, 154
Antidosis, 44
Antiphon, the orator, 112
Anytus, 37
Apaturia, 134
Appeal: under Solon, 3, 30; from council to courts, 14, 17, 40; from courts, 33, 45; against tribute, 45, 175; abuses of, 46
Arbitration: made obligatory, 26; in libel suits, 71; public, 94; held in temples, 145
Archon: functions of, 2, 15, 16, 133, 139; chosen from Zeugitae and Thetes, 10; annual term of, 28; proclamation of, 28
Areopagus: development from Homeric Council of Elders, 2, 34;

weakened by Cleisthenes, 6; opposed to democracy, 8; supremacy of, 8; attacked by Ephialtes and Pericles, 9, 50, 63; favored by Isocrates, 10; as homicide court, 29, 34; as *censor morum*, 32; loss of political and judicial powers, 34
Arginusae, battle of, 36, 78
Aristides: "the Just," 7; originated pay for state service, 37; assessed tribute, 45, 161; proposed collection of people in city, 47
Aristion, 3
Aristocracy: institution of in Athens, 2; ideals of public service of, 91
Aristophanes: prosecution of, 124; themes of, 126
Aristophon, 43, 64
Asclepius, cult of, 142 ff.
Aspasia: trial of, 35, 65; marriage of, to Lysicles, 56
Assembly: in Heroic Age, 2; judicial power of, 6, 22, 32, 34, 77, 84; under Cleisthenes, 6–8; increased powers of, 10; sovereign meeting of, 18; agenda of other meeting, 18; membership of, 47–48; pay for attendance, 11, 57, 98; leaders in, 50; experts in, 51; irresponsibility of, 69; order in, 74; intolerance of, 75; disorders in, 75; deception of, 76; impeachment before, 84
Assessors, 13
Athena, patron goddess, 137
Athens: self-sufficiency of, 104; "School of Hellas," 108, 173, 176; festivals of, 137; an imperial city, 159
Atimia. See Disfranchisement
Attica, unification of, 2, 132
Audit: of assessors, 14; dishonesty in, 15; of ambassadors, 21; of officials, 60

WESTMAR COLLEGE LIBRARY